I0815614

the FOUR CONNECTIONS

the FOUR CONNECTIONS

How to Flourish by Aligning Your

BELIEFS, BODY, BRAIN, and BONDS

Anne Kertz Kernion

LoyolaPress.
A Jesuit Ministry

LOYOLA PRESS.
A JESUIT MINISTRY
www.loyolapress.com

Cover art credit: Anne Kertz Kernion, PaulMaguire/iStock/Getty Images
Author photo credit: Mercedes Jones Photography

ISBN: 978-0-8294-5627-1
Library of Congress Control Number: 2025947388

Published in Chicago, IL
Printed in the United States of America
25 26 27 28 29 30 31 32 33 34 Versa 10 9 8 7 6 5 4 3 2 1

Dedicated to my grandchildren Morgan, Percy, Milly, Sawyer, Mack, and Charlie, who nourish my heart, renew my hope, and fill me with joy.

CONTENTS

INTRODUCTION

People say that what we're all seeking is a meaning for life. I don't think that's what we're really seeking. I think that what we're seeking is an experience of being alive, so that our life experiences on the purely physical plane will have resonances with our own innermost being and reality, so that we actually feel the rapture of being alive.

—Joseph Campbell

How can we feel the rapture of being alive, more connected to others, happier and healthier? That is exactly the question I will answer in the pages ahead. We often hear the advice: "Change your mind, change your life." But that's just the first step toward wholeness, happiness, and flourishing. There's so much more to creating the life you desire. Based on emerging insights from neuroscience and psychology that dovetail with ancient spiritual practices, we find avenues to health that can improve our lives in remarkable ways.

Inside these chapters, you'll find practices to transform your entire experience of living. I don't offer one specific approach to wellness, but explore the different aspects that contribute to health and well-being: physical, mental, cognitive, and spiritual, while considering how these dimensions interconnect and influence one another. This book presents a new approach, completely reimagining personal growth instead of merely making small adjustments at the edges. My hope is that it changes how you think about developing and flourishing. Because when we view these particulars from a bird's-eye-view, we clearly see that everything is interrelated. By drawing attention and awareness to these deep connections, our lives can be reshaped for the better.

First, we'll see how our mindset and beliefs influence how we handle daily stressors and challenges, improving our health or harming it. For example, our attitudes about stress can either send us into a frazzled state or provide us with energized determination. Additionally, and incredibly, our thoughts about our health and lifespan can steer us towards better or worse outcomes, depending on our mental inclinations. You'll find many examples in these pages, covering a range of beliefs. So yes, thoughts *do* matter! In fact, business magnate Henry Ford has been credited with saying, "Whether you think you can, or you think you can't, you are usually right." And now, we have the research to prove his point.

But what else? We also explore how much our relationships and connections drive positive physical, cognitive, and emotional benefits. Our ancestors lived in tight communities, relying on one another to survive and thrive. We humans living in the twenty-first century are also built for this kind of interdependence, perhaps more than we ever realized. If we want to retain health and deep-down happiness over our lifespan, nurturing our relationships is absolutely essential, as we will see.

Third, I can confidently predict that maintaining brain health is of uppermost importance to every person reading this book. We will uncover many strategies that help maintain and enhance cognitive skills, through thoughts, habits, and diets. I think you'll be amazed how impactful little tweaks to the daily routine can boost your brain health for years to come. It's not magic, but it's astounding how much control we have over preserving mental sharpness.

Finally, we'll examine how to care for these bodies of ours in the best way possible. Some of the most enlightening recent discoveries show the connections between brain health, psychological well-being, and gut health. Yes, all aspects of our beings are amazingly intertwined, and we ignore these connections at our peril.

Each one of these areas—the body, brain, bonds, and beliefs—influences the others. When we undertake positive practices in one, we influence the others in helpful ways. In this book, you'll discover real-world strategies to improve your relationships, your mental and cognitive health, and your physical well-being, while learning methods to navigate challenges and build resilience.

I am deeply passionate about health, and about motivating others to implement practices that can promote wellness. Why? Because I have experienced the cascading effects of healthy habits, with the accompanying joy and aliveness that attaches to them. Now, let me be clear: I am *far* from perfect in every area of health. (Just ask my family.) But I'm absolutely fascinated by the latest scientific research into how we can maximize our actions to help us improve our lives, be of service to others, and live out our beliefs as best we can.

An entrepreneur for over forty years and a wellness instructor and workshop leader, I provide insights to nourish wholeness and balance to groups around the country, and I see how impactful these messages are to those I meet. Throughout this book, you'll find simple practices to follow and implement, bringing greater balance, health, and positivity to your life. Along the way, I'm hopeful that learning about the neuroscience and psychological research underlying each practice will lend weight and motivation to encourage you to sample and embrace a few of the recommended practices.

So my aspiration is that you, dear reader, will find this information useful and enormously helpful for your mind and body. I truly want you to feel more connected to others, more purposeful and needed, and motivated to move your body to gain both mental and physical benefits, challenging your brain so it serves you well into your later years. Thank you for joining me on this journey that aims, for each of us, to "feel the rapture of being alive."

PART I

BELIEFS

MINDSETS

Reality is created by the mind; we can change our reality by changing our mind.

—Plato

Beliefs are more powerful than we imagine. I'd like to share a story of how my errant beliefs at age twenty-two almost cost me the love of my life. I'll explain, but bear with me. It's a long story.

I met Jack on a Thursday night—October 2, 1980, to be exact—at folk group practice at Pennsylvania State University. I played guitar and sang in the group the previous academic year, and Jack joined us in the fall of 1980. Jack was wearing a T-shirt from the Pittsburgh Great Race, which he had completed the previous Sunday. I asked about the event and his time for the 10K distance. When he said, "32:17," I was quite impressed. I had run a few 26-mile marathons, slowly. I simply enjoyed the challenge and the solitude of the training runs. Jack also played guitar, so we stood next to each other alongside the third guitarist. Following that first practice, he asked if I'd like to take a run together. "Of course," I said, and we agreed to meet in a few days. I remember parts of that run vividly. First, he let me set the pace, thank goodness. He was fine with that, since I could never match his speed, and I noted his kindness and thoughtfulness. We ran through the farmland around Beaver Stadium, and during our conversation, Jack mentioned that he had just exited a long-term relationship. Since I was a year older, I believed I could offer him advice. Two things I got wrong here: One, I had never been in a serious relationship, so what did I know? And two, why would being a year older confer any relationship wisdom upon me? But no, I believed I could "help" him, and so I said, "Take your time getting into another relationship." As soon as those words left my lips, I regretted them. I thought to myself, *What if I wind up liking this guy and I just told him to back off?* However, I was on my way to Chile with the Maryknoll Lay Missioners and my friend Mary the following year and wasn't looking for a boyfriend.

The weeks and months passed that fall of my senior year, and Jack and I became fast friends. Not "fast" in running terms, but close in spirit. We regularly ran together, played racquetball almost weekly, and saw each other at folk group practice and Saturday Mass. I looked forward to the post-practice/Mass gatherings, making sure I sat next to Jack every chance I got. I didn't get a sense that he viewed me as anything other than a good friend. He mentioned a girl in his engineering class once, so I assumed they were dating. I certainly was not going to stick my neck out and take a chance on being rejected.

A week before Christmas, we went out to Roy Rogers for dinner. Big spenders we were! Jack presented me with a new running watch and gave me a hug. As Jack tells it, I should have figured out then that he considered me more than a friend, but my belief about his dating status kept me from thinking that. I thanked him for his generosity and wished him a merry Christmas.

I drove home to St. Louis and, all during the holiday break, told my mom about this great guy I met. "We have so much in common, Mom, and I love spending time with him. I just wish I could put him in a bottle so he would be waiting for me when I return from Chile." But that was making the big assumption that he was interested in me, which I didn't believe was true. Jack would report that he invited me to the movies in October, but I declined his offer since I was heading to a retreat. He took that as a sign I had no interest in dating him and never asked again. I took his lack of asking again as a sign that he wanted to just be friends.

We returned to campus the first week of January, and Jack and I began spending as much time together as possible. Of course, as engineering students, we had plenty of studying to do. I also thought Jack was working with this other girl during those times, yet I couldn't stop thinking about him. Graduation loomed ahead, and I began to dread the thought of leaving State College and Jack. The time to find out if this friendship could become something more was shrinking fast.

With each passing day, I continued to learn what a wonderful human being he was. Compassionate, intelligent, and caring—everything I could hope for in a lifelong partner. By late January, I realized I loved him deeply. Of course I didn't tell him. I thought he had a girlfriend! When I look back on those days, it's hard to imagine how I thought he would be spending time with this other girl when he spent so many hours with me. But I held onto that belief, even in the face of strong evidence to the contrary. On Valentine's Day, a Saturday, I was scheduled to drive to Maryknoll, New York, to take their required psychological test. I asked Jack if he'd like to go for an early run before I left. "Sure," he said, and we ran about four miles around the golf course. I returned to the house I shared with my roommates, who all teased me about my Valentine's Day running "date." They seemed to know something I didn't.

I passed the psychological test, so the path to Chile was now clear. My heart was filled with joy, but also a painful, deep longing for more days with Jack. About a week before the end of the term, we stayed up late one night talking, and I decided to (kind of) spill the beans. Steeling myself for rejection, I told him how I hoped that he would still be around when I returned from Chile in three years. He didn't say anything in response, so I figured my belief about his girlfriend was true. (I later discovered that Jack is not a late-night kind of guy.

He said he was groggy and wasn't sure he heard me correctly, so didn't respond to my statement.)

Okay, I thought. I will still enjoy every moment we could spend together. Two days before I would drive home, our folk group threw a graduation party for me. After singing and dancing together all night, we crashed on the floor and couches. I was next to Jack, and as I was falling asleep, I threw caution to the wind and blurted out, "I love you." He turned to face me and said, "Me, too!" and we shared our first kiss. He then said, "I'll wait for you until you return from Chile." I was stunned and elated. My beliefs about him had been all wrong. He didn't have a girlfriend. And he had fallen in love with me, too. But he had believed my desire to serve in Chile meant I wasn't interested in him as a boyfriend. Boy, were we a pair!

There are a few morals to this story, but the most salient one is that beliefs are powerful. They can cloud our thinking, influence our actions, and change the course of our lives. Let's explore the power of beliefs and their impacts. I think you'll be quite surprised by how much they influence our bodily functions and our overall well-being.

Our bodies are amazingly complex, and we walk around all day unaware of the myriad processes going on below the surface of our skin. (And sometimes even *at* the surface of our skin.) Our brains and bodies communicate all day long, and the connections between them are more intricate than we could ever imagine.

One of the most recent scientific discoveries is that what we believe strongly impacts how our bodies act and react. You and I may not be surprised by these findings because we've experienced this connection many times, in various ways. For example, we may be invited to give a speech at a family gathering, or we need to initiate a difficult conversation with a friend or business associate. An hour beforehand, we might notice our bodies getting ready for the talk: Our heart rates speed up, our palms get sweaty, and our stomachs feel a bit queasy. By simply thinking about the task, our brains are preparing our bodies.

But when these physical reactions are too strong, they are not at all helpful, causing us distress as we try to get our nerves under control.

I had plenty of those proverbial butterflies the night of my graduation party, as I tried to muster the courage to finally tell Jack how much I loved him. Although to be honest, I hadn't allowed myself to imagine this outcome and how happy I would be. I remember thinking, *Anne, what do you have to lose? Your pride? And what do you have to gain? That perhaps Jack will confirm his love for you, too?* I had to overcome my anxiousness, because the upside was way more positive than any possible downside.

We have a choice when it comes to these important events. We can fret about being tense, perhaps thinking that our nervousness means it's more likely that we'll mess up and stumble over our words. Those thoughts mean you'll probably have a more difficult time performing at your very best. The second option is to tell ourselves something like: "My body is helping me prepare for this speech, which is an honor and opportunity that is important to me. This heightened awareness means my mind will be at its best." The greatest way to use stress to our advantage is to think of it as an ally, helping us succeed.[1]

Belief effects occur when information changes a person's biology or psychology. For example, if I believe that a certain food is indulgent, the amount of the hormone ghrelin released in my stomach decreases. Less ghrelin equals less hunger. So the more we believe our food is satisfying, the less hungry we feel. That is a belief effect.

One of the most fascinating studies on belief effects was conducted by Alia Crum and Ellen Langer at Harvard. They recruited hotel housekeepers and asked if they regularly exercised. The group did not believe they exercised at all. But half of the group were informed that their work—that is, making beds, vacuuming, and cleaning rooms all day long—actually did qualify as exercise. The other half received no new information; specifically, they did not learn that their work was, in fact, exercise.

After four weeks, the informed group had measurable improvements in their physical health: lower blood pressure, lower body weight, and decreased body fat. All these benefits were due to the simple change in mindset that they believed their daily tasks qualified as exercise. The control group saw no change in their markers of physical health.[2] What any of us believe about our lives, our activities, and other people will directly affect our minds, bodies, and actions. As you already saw, I created an entire narrative around Jack and his engineering classmate and based my thoughts and actions on that errant belief.

An important aspect of our beliefs as they relate to health is how we view stress. If we believe that stress is debilitating, it will cause us difficulty and, as a result, we may avoid certain activities. I have a friend who has panic attacks before she boards an airplane, so she hasn't flown in a few years. I can sympathize, because years ago, I became a very nervous flyer, due to a close call our college volleyball team experienced on a small commuter flight. We were flying from Minnesota to Missouri and encountered severe turbulence, losing elevation quickly. The two flight attendants began screaming and ran to the back of the plane, causing us to panic as well. My teammates and I, mostly Catholic girls, held hands and began praying. Obviously, since I'm retelling the story, we landed safely. But I'm probably not the only one who faced some aftereffects from the incident.

Years later, when I began flying frequently to conferences, I mentally prepared myself to die in a crash every single time I traveled. I packed my bags with a heavy heart, thinking that it was possible I'd never see my family again—I kid you not! I built a whole narrative around my one frightful flying experience, and expected the same drama, or worse, to occur every time thereafter. So when I flew, at the slightest tilt of the plane, I would put a death grip on the armrest while my heart rate and breathing quickened. It was exhausting, and I longed to be one of those people who calmly read a book during takeoff and turbulence. You might notice a pattern here: I was a champion at clinging to beliefs, whether it was about Jack and his nonexistent girlfriend or about the danger of air travel.

After a few years of this illogical behavior and the toll it was taking on me, I decided to read about air travel safety and discovered breathing techniques to calm myself before takeoff. I read about how flying is statistically much safer than driving to the airport, and now I am able to relax and read during most turbulent events. I was able to change that belief through educating myself, just like the hotel cleaning staff once they learned that their work was, in fact, exercise.

> *Stress is not what happens to us. It's our response to what happens. And response is something we can choose.*
>
> —Maureen Killoran

Adopting a positive attitude toward your stress allows it to serve you, instead of negatively impacting you. When facing an intimidating scenario, ask yourself: What do I have to gain, and what do I have to lose if I proceed? Keep those thoughts in mind and allow your answers to change your attitude and how your body reacts to the stressors. Practice this every time you feel anxious about a situation, and you might even begin welcoming these experiences. At the very least, you will become a pro at handling stress. As renowned psychologist William James observed, "Human beings, by changing the inner attitudes of their minds, can change the outer aspects of their lives."

PLACEBOS

The placebo effect isn't some mysterious response to a sugar pill. It is the robust and measurable effect of three components: the body's natural ability to heal, the patient mindset, and the social context.

—Dr. Alia Crum

The placebo effect occurs when beliefs interact with an inert substance and we see a positive outcome. Why is this an important idea? Because what we believe about our health, about medications we are taking and treatments we are receiving, will affect the efficacy of those interventions. If you believe that the physical therapist or chiropractor is helping relieve your pain and discomfort, the treatment will be more effective. If you believe that a pill is having a positive effect on your health, it is likely that your attitude will amplify the medication's positive effects.

A fascinating study on the interplay of beliefs and health was led by Harvard professor Ted Kaptchuk, a leading medical researcher of placebos. Our paths crossed years ago when I chauffeured him to the high school where my husband was leading a seminar for the science department. Little did I know that my future interests would align with his area of expertise. Professor Kaptchuk's placebo study explored how people reacted to migraine pain medication. A migraine drug, labeled with the drug's name, was given to one group. A placebo (just a sugar pill) labeled *Placebo* was given to a second group, and the third group did not receive anything. Remarkably, the placebo was 50% as effective as the migraine drug to reduce pain after a migraine attack.

The researchers hypothesized that the act of taking a pill was enough to cause this reduction in pain. "People associate the ritual of taking medicine as a positive healing effect," says Kaptchuk. "Even if they know it's not medicine, the action itself can stimulate the brain into thinking the body is being healed."[3] At the completion of one study on placebos, the patients asked to continue taking the sugar pill, even though they knew it was just a sugar pill, which I find particularly amusing, but also insightful.

How can we duplicate the placebo effect without taking a fake pill? By caring for our minds and bodies, says Kaptchuk. Eat a healthy diet, exercise, stretch, socialize, meditate. All these self-care practices provide some of the key ingredients of the placebo effect. And the level of attention we give to these practices can enhance their benefits.

It's important to understand that placebos work for some ailments, but not for others. We can't fix a broken bone, cure cancer, or lower cholesterol through placebos. We can, however, lessen perceived pain, as well as other medical conditions. Depression, fatigue, allergies, irritable bowel syndrome, Parkinson's disease, and even osteoarthritis of the knee are a few of the conditions that respond positively to placebos.

Even when taking drugs for a sickness, our expectations for healing will influence the outcome. When we receive information about a drug or a therapy, we may come to expect that if we take that drug or perform the therapy, we will improve. That expectation activates certain neural circuits in the brain that impact our immune systems, our nervous systems, our respiratory systems, our cardiovascular systems, etc. We can actually help our bodies heal by enlisting our minds to offer some assistance along the way.[4]

Many people reinforce their hope for a good outcome by performing little rituals before a performance or competition. My dad coached our Catholic grade-school basketball team, and before each game, he insisted we stand in a circle, stretch our arms out to touch one another's hands in the center, and recite the Hail Mary in unison. We were an intense group of girls praying for a win, plain and simple. But Dad also hoped that this short ritual would calm our nerves as we sought a Catholic League championship. On the Sunday of the title game, we took our prayer ritual up a notch and attended Mass together as a team. We were playing St. Margaret of Scotland, a team that had beaten us by thirty points earlier in the season, and we needed all the help we could get. We played a great game but lost by just one point. We were very disappointed, of course, but proud of our improvement and pleased we had given them a run for their money. We believed we could win, and almost accomplished that goal. I can't say for sure if our pregame rituals helped our cause, but they certainly didn't hurt.

As an adult, I didn't perform any specific rituals before my running events. In our twenties, Jack and I often competed in the same road races. We would jog a bit to warm up, and every time we lined up on the starting line, Jack would say, "I know you're going to do great, Anne. I'll see you at the finish line." Although road races aren't on my scorecard anymore, Jack voices the same affirmation right before I give an important presentation. It is quite calming and uplifting to have someone encourage you and believe in you.

DID YOU KNOW?

Many athletes believe pregame rituals will boost their level of play. Pittsburgh Penguins hockey star Sidney Crosby is known to have numerous pregame rituals and superstitions. When asked to talk about them, he replied, "How much time do you have?" For example, he never talks to his mother on game days, since he has been injured several times after speaking with her. Crosby also requires that his hockey sticks be cut to a specific length and taped in a very specific way. He does not allow anyone else to touch them afterwards or he will re-tape them himself. He believes that these rituals help maintain his superb hockey skills. And although we might think they are silly or useless, research has shown that these rituals produce benefits such as increased confidence, which improves performance.[5]

Our mindsets and attitudes directly influence our physical and mental health in powerful ways. The beliefs we hold can help us handle stress better, enhance our well-being, and even change how well medical treatments work for us. Understanding this strong connection between mind and body arms us with helpful tools to improve our everyday lives and strengthen our overall health.

AWE AND WONDER

I think my proper response is complete amazement and awe at the universe that we are in.

—John C. Mather

Awe is defined by Dacher Keltner, PhD, as the "feeling of being in the presence of something vast that transcends your current understanding of the world." Keltner studies the impact of awe and how experiencing it contributes to our psychological and physical well-being.[6] Awe is a universal human experience, found in every culture around the globe. Can you guess what the most common portal for experiencing awe is? It's not money, status, or anything materialistic. It is the kindness, courage, or strength we witness in other people that most frequently creates the feeling of awe. Turns out we humans are gobsmacked by people who exhibit exceptional virtue, character, and goodness. As I was getting to know Jack, his kindness, gentleness, and awareness of others kept surprising and delighting me. I didn't care a lick about whether he had a car, or status, or money. The thought never occurred to me. Day in and day out, I observed a young man possessing extraordinary integrity and goodness, and I could not help being captivated by him.

I also recall my fellow Pittsburgher and hero, Mister Rogers, whose goodness and gentle spirit modeled how to be a compassionate, soulful human being. (I cherish a handwritten note from him, framed and hanging in our home, congratulating me for the beautiful messages contained on my greeting cards. He bought them regularly at a gift shop within walking distance of his studio.) Mister Rogers's centered presence evoked awe in millions, teaching all of us, in very simple ways, how to be better human beings.

> *In its encounter with Nature, science invariably elicits a sense of reverence and awe. The very act of understanding is a celebration of joining, merging, even if on a very modest scale, with the magnificence of the Cosmos.*
>
> —Carl Sagan

Jack experienced spine-tingling awe when he watched his former AP Physics student Woody Hoburg pilot the NASA/SpaceX Crew-6 rocket. It launched from the Kennedy Space Center to the International Space Station in early 2023. Jack attended as one of Woody's guests and remarked that witnessing the ship's liftoff was a highlight of a lifetime. He was awestruck in two ways: by the magnificent engineering feat that can launch a spacecraft into orbit, and also by the young man inside, whom he knew as an extraordinarily talented, dedicated, kind, humble human being. Knowing he played a small part in Woody's education and development made him happy and proud. To Jack, it seemed only a few years ago that he had watched teenage Woody launch a rocket he had designed. Jack and our son Jackson remember standing in a grassy field as the homemade rocket soared above their heads. Little did they know this launch was a sign of bigger things to come.

Later in the summer of 2023, while Woody was still in space, he emailed Jack with greetings and a picture of himself on a spacewalk outside the International Space Station. Two "awe moments" deserve extra attention: the astounding photo of Woody showing Earth in the far background, and the astonishing fact that we can email from outer space!

One of the most surprising things I learned from Woody's adventure in space is that the astronauts can place orders for deliveries. One week, I read that the crew was anticipating the arrival of a supply rocket carrying replenishments. I assumed they would request repair parts or fuel or whatever nuts and bolts and equipment astronauts need to do their jobs. But what did they order? Hard cheeses and fresh fruit! Yep! They have door-to-door delivery of food to the Space Station! (Can you imagine the delivery fee? And what is their address, exactly?) Even though they are 250 miles above Earth and they are moving at about five miles per second (do the math: that's 18,000 miles per hour!), they still count on us to provide what they need. Pretty cool!

However, we don't need rocket launches or photos of Earth taken from space to experience awe—although, granted, those are pretty amazing! In everyday life, it's more difficult to recognize the ordinary wonders like the sun setting on the horizon or robins chirping in nearby trees. We can also access awe through art, music, and the kindness of another human being.

> *Every moment, we have the opportunity to wake up to wonder, to awe, to everyday miracles. It is enough to make your heart leap with joy, to overwhelm your soul, if you let it. Every day, we have access to this, in so much abundance. Will you let it in?*
>
> —Leo Babauta

PRACTICE

We can tap into awe in our daily lives in a few easy ways, as suggested below.

1. **Be fully present:** A few times each day, take a deep breath and be here now. Look around, devote your full attention to the wonders you see all around you. What would your grandmother

see as amazing in this scene, this room, this situation? In all the world, with whom would you choose to share this moment?

2. **Notice nature:** Stand still and take in the beauty of a sunset, the stars and moon at night, or the flowers, shrubs, and trees in every season. How infrequently we just stop moving through our daily duties! (I'm looking in the mirror here, too.) Pause for just thirty seconds and look around. If you aren't able to get outside, immerse yourself in a video of nature to feel wonder and amazement.
3. **Observe humans:** Watch or read about someone's extraordinary kindness, or good deeds being done in communities all over the world.

> *We dismiss wonder commonly with childhood. Much later, when life's pace has slackened, wonder may return. The mind then may find so much inviting wonder, the whole world becomes wonderful. Then one thing is scarcely more wonderful than is another. But, the greatest wonder, our wonder soon lapses. A rainbow every morning, who would pause to look at it? The wonderful which comes often or is plentiful about us, is soon taken for granted. That is practical enough. It allows us to get on with life. But it may stultify if it cannot on occasion be thrown off. To recapture now and then childhood's wonder, is to secure a driving force for occasional grown-up thoughts.*
>
> —Charles Scott Sherrington

University of California researcher Virginia Sturm, PhD, found that awe experiences reduce inflammation in the body and enhance positive emotions, particularly in older adults and in people suffering with anxiety and depression. Dr. Sturm studied "awe walks," where older participants walked in nature; afterward, they were less stressed, more compassionate, and, simply put, happier. They became less focused on themselves, more socially connected, and experienced lasting positive effects on their emotional well-being.[7]

DID YOU KNOW?

Awe is associated with enhanced heart rate variability (HRV); improved digestion, immunity, and stress management; increased oxytocin release; better social connections; and reduced inflammation. All these positive outcomes are known to be beneficial to our mental and physical health and well-being.[8]

> *Our goal should be to live life in radical amazement, [to] get up in the morning and look around at the world in a way that takes nothing for granted. Everything is phenomenal. Everything is incredible. To be spiritual is to be amazed.*
>
> —Rabbi Abraham Joshua Heschel

Around 3:00 p.m. on Monday, April 8, 2024, many of us living in the United States experienced amazement as we watched the moon slowly meander its way across our view of the sun. (Wearing our protective glasses, of course.) I noticed birdsong quieting, the atmosphere becoming dim, and light occasionally poking through the clouds, casting eerie shadows on the ground.

Eclipses remind us that we are a small part of a vast, often mysterious universe. Just the reminder of our smallness makes us feel more connected to one another as well as more motivated to be connected with other people. Psychologists tell us that when humans come together over a positive shared experience, we exhibit "collective effervescence," which magnifies our emotions and boosts our sense of well-being.

Exactly how does this happen?

"People with anxiety tend to spend a lot of time in the future. And people with depression spend a lot of time in the past," says psychologist Kate Russo. Experiencing an eclipse, however, can draw us back into the present moment. "When you're less anxious and worried, it opens you up to be more attuned to other people, feel more connected, [to] care for others and be more compassionate," says Sean Goldy, a researcher at Johns Hopkins University.[9]

> *The whole world is a series of miracles, but we're so used to them that we call them everyday things.*
>
> —Hans Christian Anderson

As author and mindfulness expert Jack Kornfield, PhD, says, "It's amazing to step out of the busyness of our lives, to come back to the mystery of our own existence." Perhaps experiencing an eclipse, or any unusual natural event, helps us to remember that our universe is steeped in wonder, waiting for us to cultivate eyes to see its beauty and mystery. Experiencing awe can boost our happiness, aid in eliminating depression and some auto-immune diseases, foster kindness and creativity, lower stress levels, and lengthen life expectancy.[10] Pretty "awe-some," if you ask me!

> *When you arise in the morning, think of what a privilege it is to be alive—to breathe, to think, to enjoy, to love—then make that day count!*
>
> —Steve Maraboli

PRAYER

Prayer is a small fire lit to keep cold hands warm. Prayer is a practice that flourishes both with faith and doubt. Prayer is asking, and prayer is sitting. Prayer is the breath. Prayer is not an answer, always, because not all questions can be answered.

—Pádraig Ó Tuama

My maternal grandmother was one of my favorite people. Grandma Gessner was widowed in her mid-forties, forcing her to return to work as a nurse while raising six children as a single mother. Several years later, her youngest daughter died from cancer at the age of twenty-one. I cannot imagine the grief and sadness she bore due to those losses, yet she soldiered on with calm determination. She very rarely mentioned religion, but the evidence—crosses, medals, a Bible, pictures of saints—were everywhere throughout her home. She kept a well-worn rosary hanging from her bedpost. Anyone could see that spirituality was important to her. Whenever I read about the many benefits of praying the rosary, I think of Grandma. I'm sure her practice provided solace and support as she struggled to stay afloat both financially and psychologically after her husband, and then daughter, died so young. I carry her rosary beads in my computer bag as a reminder of her quiet spirituality and the way she lived with genuine joy, even in the face of great trials.

I learned so much from Grandma, but she did not preach or provide explicit lessons for us to digest. A woman of action and few words, Grandma lived in a three-room trailer near the St. Louis airport, and I occasionally spent the night with her. It was a very different atmosphere from the suburban house where I was raised. Her mobile home, furnished as it was with outdated furniture, was quite modest. The knickknacks on her shelves rattled when planes came in for a landing or took off from the airport. But I treasured the simplicity of her home. When I was there, I felt surrounded by warmth and love.

> *We do not know how long we will live, but this not knowing calls us to live every day, every week, every year of our lives to its fullest potential.*
>
> —Henri Nouwen

Grandma may not have known about theologian and writer Henri Nouwen, or read any of his words, but her life was a shining example of his ideas. She visited our home often to babysit me and my siblings, arriving with her wide smile and gifts of what she called "junk food," which were rare treats for her grandchildren. She would open the bags of chips and Cheetos and we would sit with her at our kitchen table, sharing stories about school and sports and friends and homework. Grandma would eventually pick up the assorted socks we had set aside for her hands, darning them with needle and thread, magically making them new again. Some of my favorite memories were the nights she allowed us to stay up past our bedtime and watch scary movies, something our parents forbade. When we heard the garage door opening, she'd shoo us into our bedrooms and we'd pretend to be fast asleep. We kept that secret for many, many years, and I still laugh about it today.

Simply put, Grandma lived with a *joie de vivre*, and I'm certain her spunk rubbed off on me. She told the story of how in 1918, at the age of twenty, she boarded a train bound for the "big city" of Minneapolis to attend nursing school. Imagine that! She most likely experienced both excitement and nervousness as she set out on such a journey, but her inner strength and steely determination, qualities I admire most, were clearly part of her character throughout her entire life. She lived to the age of ninety, grateful to the end for a life that was both full and long.

Only in my adult years did I begin to ponder the effects of her daily prayer practices on her resilience and overall well-being. As a young girl, I took for granted Grandma's strength and steadfastness. But as I grew older and contemplated the source of her hardiness, I came to realize that her rosary beads could tell quite a story if they could talk.

Grandma would not have been surprised to hear about a recent study exploring the effects of praying the rosary on health and well-being. The participants in the study felt peace, contentment, and a connection with the divine as a result of their prayers. Praying the rosary helped participants handle difficult life events, cultivating acceptance, humbleness, and devotion.[11]

DID YOU KNOW?

One study showed that praying the rosary—specifically, saying the Hail Mary—or chanting a yoga mantra produced breathing rates of around six per minute. This is the exact number of inspirations that scientists find is best for heart health, as it maximizes our heart rate variability. Heart rate variability is associated with better stress resilience and overall health. This breathing rate also reduces anxiety and cortisol, stabilizes blood pressure, and promotes calm and relaxation. So we might want to choose one of those ancient practices if we hope to boost our HRV.[12]

The Daily Examen is a five-hundred-year-old prayer practice popularized by Ignatius of Loyola. It is a simple exercise done in the evening, the purpose of which is to reflect on the positive aspects of the day, let go of any negative emotions, and notice, sense, or be more aware of the presence of God.

I've spoken with a Duke University professor who has led research into the Examen's positive benefits for managing stress for ministers. Since members of the clergy typically experience high rates of mental and physical health challenges, Duke partnered with United Methodist clergy in North Carolina to evaluate four stress management practices, one of them being the Daily Examen. One group of clergy members practiced the Examen for ten to fifteen minutes, on most days, for six months. Compared to a control group, the Examen group experienced significantly less stress reactivity and anxiety symptoms; they also reported increased spiritual well-being in their ministries. The professor's research team found that practicing the Examen regularly helped improve depression symptoms.[13]

Another study looked at two interventions, the Examen and mindfulness, to train addiction treatment patients as part of their recovery. Briefly stated, mindfulness is being aware of our thoughts and feelings and accepting them without judgment. It is simply being here now, paying attention to what we are experiencing in the present moment, without rehashing the past or worrying about the future. In the chapters ahead, we will continue exploring the myriad benefits of mindfulness. The researchers found that Examen practitioners had similar reductions as the mindfulness group on depression, anxiety, and stress, and had better results with curbing their substance cravings.[14] These studies show that this ancient prayer practice holds promise in treating these important mental health issues. I offer a small daily Examen card on my website.[15]

Baylor University researchers discovered that one's beliefs about the character of God can determine the effects of prayer on mental health. People who pray to a loving and protective God are less likely to experience anxiety-related disorders compared to people who pray to a judgmental God. Those anxiety issues include worry, fear, self-consciousness, social anxiety, and obsessive-compulsive behavior. When God is seen as a source of comfort and strength, people praying feel supported emotionally, experience fewer symptoms of anxiety disorders, and see increased resilience.[16]

One simple prayer practice, loving-kindness meditation, cultivates compassion towards ourselves and others, with proven psychological and physical benefits.

PRACTICE

Cross your arms over your heart and close your eyes.

1. **Begin by sending loving thoughts toward yourself:** *May I be happy. May I be healthy. May I be safe. May my heart be at peace.*

2. **Then extend these well-wishes towards loved ones:** *May they be happy. May they be healthy. May they be safe. May their hearts be at peace.*

3. **And finally, send those thoughts to:** neutral people, then difficult persons, then to all people.

Some of the specific benefits found from practicing loving-kindness meditation include:

- an increase in positive emotions, life satisfaction, and better social connections;[17]

- a reduction in stress, anxiety, and inflammation;[18] and

- enhanced empathy, compassion for others, and emotional regulation.[19]

This easy practice can be taught to young children and older adults alike, accruing great benefits for each. Just think of the positive effects on our world if all of us spent a few minutes each day sending compassionate thoughts to others. Another practice comes from the Quakers, who "hold someone in the Light." It is a form of prayer in which someone is held in God's illuminating presence and love.

Prayer is a difficult practice to study rigorously, due to many constraints. But a few scientific studies have shown the benefits of praying, including several that my grandma must have experienced.[20]

- **Reduces stress.** Prayer helps many people deal with the difficulties of life by off-loading worry to a higher being. Daily stressors affect our mood and our health, and praying can both boost hope and lessen strain. Research shows that those people who pray often feel less pain, they tend to be less reactive to negative events, and they become angry less frequently.[21]

- **Lowers risk of depression.** A few studies on religion and depression found that women and men whose religion or spirituality is highly important to them have about one-fourth the risk of experiencing major depression compared with people who are not spiritual. Interestingly, this result did not depend on religious service attendance or religious denomination; however, the frequency of prayer predicted lowered depression, less anxiety, fewer post-traumatic stress disorders (PTSD), less substance abuse, and greater self-esteem. The research determined that meditation and other spiritual practices—*when engaged in on a regular basis*—lead to a thickening of the brain's cortex. The relatively thicker cortex was found in precisely the same regions of the brain that had otherwise shown thinning in people who were at a high risk for depression. In other words, prayer and meditation have a protective effect on the brain.[22]

So if you, your friends, or loved ones have struggled with bouts of depression, adding one of these spiritual practices may help alleviate some of the suffering.[23]

- **Helps maintain a positive outlook on life.**[24] Many religious traditions recommend gratitude practices, and these alone can help practitioners maintain a positive mindset. No matter what our daily struggles may be, we can be thankful we are alive. Or, as a friend once said, we can be grateful we are six feet over the ground instead of six feet under. We can nurture gratitude *in* our situation, even if we are not particularly grateful *for* the situation. This "attitude of gratitude" changes one's outlook on life for the better.[25]

- **Good for your heart.** Prayer, like other forms of meditation, can boost heart health by lowering stress, heart rate, and blood pressure. It also often lowers cortisol levels and boosts heart rate variability. Cardiac patients using gratitude journals have better cardiovascular outcomes than cardiac patients who do not.[26]

- **Increases lifespan.** Because prayer often minimizes stress and anxiety, it can boost the body's immune system, helping us fight illness and disease. Brain MRIs showed thicker cortices in subjects who placed a high importance on religion or spirituality than those who did not.[27]

- **Improves attitude.** One recent study found that contemplative prayer increased subjects' positive emotions as well as their emotional regulation.[28] The subjects were able to handle the ups and downs of life quite well and had a lowered risk for depression and less cognitive decline. When praying in community, most people discover their troubles are minor compared to the troubles of others. My friend Marianne relayed a story of attending a church service. The priest asked each person to imagine placing their burdens in a pile. Then everyone was invited to randomly pick up someone else's burden. He then posed the question, "Would you blindly trade your problems for another's?" Most of us would decline the offer because our problems are usually much smaller than many others.

- **Alters levels of melatonin and serotonin.** Melatonin helps us fall asleep, while serotonin helps us feel awake and alive. Studies have shown that mindfulness meditation and yoga can positively affect our circadian rhythms by regulating these two neurotransmitters. We are then able to fall asleep more easily and feel more energized when awake.[29]

As we have seen, prayer can benefit our health and well-being in several ways. Similar to the benefits of meditation, regular prayer practices are associated with reduced stress levels, lower blood pressure, and improved psychological well-being. Those who pray experience connection, comfort, and more meaning in their lives. Prayer also fosters relaxation and emotional equilibrium, potentially alleviating symptoms of anxiety and depression. Finally, since prayer is often practiced in community settings, practitioners often enjoy valuable social networks that support positive outcomes for physical and mental health.

AGING

For age is opportunity no less
Than youth itself, though in another dress,
And as the evening twilight fades away
The sky is filled with stars, invisible by day.

—Henry Wadsworth Longfellow

The most common misconception regarding aging is that cognition declines as we age. It's simply not true! We attribute memory lapses to old age all too often, but some forms of memory actually improve. For example, our general knowledge recall, which includes remembering ideas, concepts and facts, is usually better as we grow older than it is when we were younger. I doubt I'd forget that John F. Kennedy was president of the United States in 1963. Or that the moon revolves around the earth, and the earth revolves around the sun. Or that the number Pi is 3.14 and a whole lot of trailing digits.

Another kind of memory, procedural, doesn't change much at all. For instance, we don't forget how to ride a bike, type a paragraph, or bake cookies. That last one is particularly true for me. The chocolate chip cookie recipe on the back of a Nestlé's bag of chocolate chips has been embedded in my brain for more than fifty-five years. I couldn't forget it if I tried! But it is possible for a person's episodic memory to decline. That's the ability to remember things like what I ate for dinner last night, or the name of the new neighbor I met last weekend. I am particularly bad at remembering the names of characters in any movie I've seen, even if I exited the theater mere minutes before. It's as if my brain doesn't think those facts are worthy of taking up space, so it doesn't bother to commit them to memory. It's almost laughable. But it's certainly not something that concerns me. If I couldn't remember how to get home from the theater, *that* would be concerning.

Holding positive aging beliefs, however, is the key to maintaining memory. Becca Levy, PhD, a professor at Yale University, has conducted groundbreaking research into how aging beliefs affect cognitive health, and, in particular, Alzheimer's disease. She finds that the main cause of memory decline in older adults is how they think about aging, since aging beliefs can influence their memory's health and performance.[30] One large study that looked at peoples' views of aging over a thirty-eight year period found that folks who held positive aging beliefs had significantly better memory scores in old age than their peers with negative views. Many older adults would tell us that their biggest fear of aging is not being referred to as "old," but developing a cognitive disease such as Alzheimer's. If someone carries the gene APOE4 for Alzheimer's disease and holds positive aging beliefs, they are almost half as likely to develop dementia compared to people carrying the gene and holding negative aging beliefs. The "positive-aging" APOE4 carriers' risk of developing Alzheimer's was as low as that of people who did not have the gene, cutting the impact of the genetic risk by almost half.[31] That's remarkable! So inheriting the Alzheimer's gene does not mean a person will definitely develop the disease: One's beliefs about aging can hold the risk of this disease and memory loss at bay.

These findings lead me back to Grandma, who worked as a hospital floor nurse until the age of seventy-six. Imagine the physical demands and emotional ups and downs she experienced, dealing with patients of all kinds. I never once heard her complain or grumble about laboring in such a demanding job into her retirement years. She never said she was "too old" to work, but felt her years of experience allowed her to care for others quite well. That, my friends, is an example of a positive aging belief. We can ask ourselves, "What skills or insights do I bring to a situation or position that a younger person may not possess?" That's the avenue of questioning that illustrates that older members of every community still have much to contribute.

And our attitudes about aging start young. Researchers find that children as young as three have already taken in cultural messages about older adults. If my grandchildren call people as young as sixty-five "old," and say it in a disparaging tone, I remind them of the many things older people—myself included!—can do that they cannot.

How and why do positive and negative aging beliefs affect us? Negative beliefs cause the hippocampus, an area of the brain partially responsible for memory, to shrink three times as fast as it does in people with positive aging beliefs. That fact alone should stop us in our tracks. (But wait—there's more!) Several factors contribute to hippocampus downsizing, including:

1. Increased stress levels occur with negative aging beliefs. Chronic stress, the kind that lingers for months or years, causes the hippocampus to shrink, rendering it less able to form new memories. In fact, an effective way to control Alzheimer's disease is to keep stress at bay. Stress causes inflammation in the brain, paving the way for neurological disease. Positive age beliefs act as a buffer against the damaging effects of stress.

2. People who hold negative attitudes toward older adults and aging may be less likely to participate in new activities and challenges such as joining a book club or taking dance lessons. The hippocampus will decline in size and ability when mentally stimulating activities are absent from our daily lives.

3. If people believe they are too old to exercise, they may lessen their physical activity levels. Just keep moving! Jack and I can't run nearly as fast as we did when we met. (And remember, "fast" described Jack's running, but not mine.) But we can run slower, break a sweat, and still enjoy the sunshine and park environs as much as we did before. Physical exercise is a critical component in combating the effects of aging: It encourages the growth of new brain cells in the hippocampus and, at the same time, enhances memory function.

> *The chief prevention against getting old is to remain astonished.*
>
> —Kevin Kelly

According to Dr. Levy's studies, holding positive aging beliefs can increase lifespan up to seven-and-a-half-years longer than someone with negative beliefs.[32] These negative beliefs may contribute to reduced neuroplasticity, which is the brain's ability to adapt and change in response to new experiences. The hippocampus is less able to form new connections, which hampers its ability to process and use new information.

How do I implement positive aging beliefs in my life? Mainly by continuing to learn and relearn skills. For example, I've started playing the piano again, after letting the piano keys collect dust for many years. The first few weeks of practice were painful, not only for me, but for anyone within earshot. Errant notes filled the air, and I continually apologized for my mistakes. Although my fingers will never glide through challenging Mozart pieces as well as eighteen-year-old Anne, I can now play several classical compositions without causing harm to listeners. I also enjoy playing simple duets with our grandchildren, Percy and Sawyer, who will eclipse my abilities any day now. But they see their grandma delighting in music-making, so hopefully their beliefs about positive aging will be bolstered, too.

Jack and I do our best to nurture positive aging mindsets by continuing to learn and share information in our chosen fields. Jack teaches AP Physics online to young people around the world. Three years ago, he realized that his students needed a more thorough background in quantum physics than what they learned in their typical high school science classes. But Jack found that high-school-level resources on the topic were nonexistent. So he pulled together the fundamental ideas of quantum physics and created a summer enrichment course for his students. He enjoyed the process, and now conveys these complicated concepts to an appreciative teenage audience.

Likewise, every day I receive news highlighting recent scientific research from neuroscientists and positive psychologists. These interesting findings often align with the spiritual practices I explore in my workshops and retreats. Since Jack and I both enjoy learning, we are fortunate to have the opportunity to share what we discover with audiences with similar interests. But even if you aren't teaching in a formal setting, all of us have opportunities to share newly acquired knowledge with friends and family. We are more interesting conversationalists if we have something to share.

The bottom line is this: Our attitudes drive our behavior. Positively or negatively. If we *think* we are getting old and frail, we will certainly get old and frail. Conversely, if we think that age is just a number, that more time on this planet represents new opportunities to learn and grow, we will live with more energy, motivation, connectivity, and youthfulness.[33] Within reason, of course, because most sixty-five-year-old bodies do not function as well as a twenty-five-year-old body. There are some limits. But in the end, our brains and our bodies will follow our beliefs. Grandma could have wallowed in despair and grief, but she fostered a youthful mindset and found joy in the smallest moments. She didn't believe that a seventy-something nurse was too old to walk hospital floors and care for patients. She happily broke babysitting rules, to the delight of her grandchildren. Grandma laughed along with us and didn't succumb to the notion that life went downhill after a certain age. Nope! She carried her spirit of wonder and gladness into her late eighties, providing a positive aging example to all who knew her. I am so grateful for all she taught me.

Some questions for all of us to ponder include: How do we view the aging process, and do we think of it as a slow descent? Or do we imagine that our later years will be rich ones during which we share our accumulated wisdom with others and enjoy an active life with family and friends?

The work of Ellen Langer, PhD, a world-renowned expert in the field of mind-body connections, demonstrates the powerful effects of beliefs on our physical health. Her well-known "Counterclockwise" study shows that men in their late seventies and early eighties who spent one week acting as if they were twenty years younger experienced remarkable improvements in physical and mental abilities.[34] These older men gained strength, flexibility, cognitive functioning, and hearing and vision acuity. And all these gains were the result of the subjects simply thinking of themselves as being twenty years younger and changing their behaviors to align with that self-image. For *just one week*!

One of Dr. Langer's studies involved nursing home residents. Some were given greater choice and responsibility over their daily lives, including caring for a houseplant. Members of the other group were each given a houseplant, but theirs were cared for by staff. After eighteen months, the "choice and responsibility" group exhibited better overall health and well-being, less depression, and greater happiness.

Dr. Langer points to many other studies that support her thesis that our health and well-being are more dependent on our beliefs than anything else.[35] One project discovered that the perception of time has an effect on the speed with which wounds heal. When clocks were sped up in recovery rooms, the patients believed more time had passed than it actually had, and the participants' wounds healed faster. When the clocks were adjusted to proceed more slowly, wound healing took more time.[36]

DID YOU KNOW?

Walking speed has been shown to be a meaningful marker of aging. One study determined that providing participants with negative aging stereotypes before they walked produced slower walking speeds. Furthermore, these slower walking speeds indicate a greater likelihood of future disabilities and hospitalizations. This shows once again that what we think and believe about ourselves will affect our abilities and our behavior. If we believe that aging is a downhill slide that is out of our control, then downhill we will go. In contrast, people who felt they had agency exercised more, maintained healthier diets, and visited the doctor more regularly. In fact, one large study with over nine hundred participants showed that having a purpose in life protected against having, or developing, a slow walking speed.[37]

Interestingly, super agers maintain the cortical thickness of their aMCC (anterior midcingulate cortex) brain region incredibly well. The measured thickness was statistically equivalent to that of young adults in their twenties and thirties. What denotes a "super ager?" Someone who exhibits brainpower similar to a person decades younger: usually physically active, a lifelong learner with excellent memory, with strong social connections and relationships. Super agers hold positive attitudes about aging. They relish challenges of all sorts. To super agers, just because they're getting older doesn't mean that life is no longer exciting and stimulating.

Our son's late grandmother-in-law, an intelligent, delightful woman who lived to the age of ninety-seven, was an inspiration to me. I met Rosemary when she was in her late eighties, when both of us attended graduation celebrations in Cambridge, Massachusetts. I was immediately impressed with her quick mind and delightful sense of humor. She had no trouble maintaining the brisk pace of our group as we walked to various events. I discovered that she continued to meet regularly with former colleagues and young friends in Oxford, England. A few years later, during our son and her granddaughter's wedding weekend, Rosemary invited me to breakfast at a local diner. She insisted on paying the bill, stating, "Please don't deny me the pleasure of treating you."

Rosemary was a conscientious person, a trait strongly associated with lengthy lifespans. "Conscientiousness, or how organized and disciplined you are, is the trait most related to longevity," says David Watson, former professor of personality psychology at University of Notre Dame. Simply put, people who are very conscientious take care of themselves better than people who aren't. The former eat a healthy diet, exercise, sleep well, don't smoke, and listen to their doctors. Basically, they are good at self-regulation and don't do stupid things. They are resilient and they bounce back from stressful situations more quickly than other people in their age group.[38]

The old adage "age is in your head" contains more truth than we ever knew. We now know that how we think about aging plays quite a significant role in how well we navigate our older years. Our mental attitudes affect everything from our cardiovascular health to our cognitive abilities. Of course, our numerical age continues marching on, but how we experience aging is influenced by our beliefs, attitudes, and mental frameworks about what aging means. So by continuing to cultivate curiosity for various dimensions of life, you'll be on your way to staying young in body, mind, and spirit.

MINDFULNESS, STRESS, AND RESILIENCE

Within you, there is a stillness and a sanctuary to which you can retreat at any time and be yourself.

—Hermann Hesse

Many of us spend our days "doing," which is to say moving from one task to the other, crossing off each line on our to-do list. If we pose the question "How are you?" to a friend or colleague, we often hear the answer, "Busy!" Of course, it feels good to be accomplishing everything we set out to do; at other times, though, we're simply exhausted. We plow through the emails, the repetitive chores, the driving to and from. The relentlessness of this pace is stressful. It wears us down physically and emotionally.

I love checking things off my list as much as anyone. But if I'm honest, I should probably do a little bit less each day and spend more time just being. That lesson hit home one night when I failed to notice—for half a day!—that my husband had substantially trimmed away his beard, a request I'd been making for a few months. I was so busy tending to my work list that his new look had gone unnoticed. So much for being present and attentive!

> *How we spend our days is, of course, how we spend our lives.*
>
> —Annie Dillard

Rick Hanson, PhD, psychologist and author, shares lessons from positive psychology and neuroscience on how to change our brains and become happier and calmer. He recommends that we examine our relationship to "doing." How can we do all of the things we need to do without feeling stressed and pressed? First, he says, take care of the high-priority things and leave the small things behind. There's an old adage, "If you're filling a bucket, put the big rocks in first." For me, that means getting to the writing of essays and designing cards before answering emails and phone messages.

Hanson also suggests engaging in activities freely and with a sense of ease. He encourages us to pay attention when we feel pressed. When this happens, he advises us to exhale deliberately, slowly, and consciously. Then we can continue the doing, but it will be done with a sense of peace. Being mindful and realizing we are pushing is the key. We can take a step back and then do just one thing at a time. Multitasking is a misnomer; we are actually task-switching, losing productivity with each switch. Focusing on one thing only will fill us with greater calm. And that's a gift we can *all* use!

Negative interactions are another source of stress because by ramping up cortisol and adrenaline they create a sense of danger. Unfortunately, these incidents are all too common. I'm thinking here of a sunny Sunday afternoon when I went for a bike ride—a favorite activity—in our local park. As I rode past a man walking in the opposite direction, for no apparent reason, he shouted at me. Immediately, my heart started pounding. I was puzzled and confused by his angry outburst. To help release the internal upset I was feeling, I began taking some slow breaths. I was able to regain the joy of my bike ride.

This is a lesson that has taken me years to learn. Sometimes all we can do is acknowledge our distress, take several deep breaths, maybe even close our eyes, (but not while bike riding!) and return to whatever we were doing. Being mindful that most of the time, people's actions and reactions have nothing to do with me is also helpful.

Resilience is a skill. We practice, over and over again, facing stressful issues calmly. When that response becomes second nature, we bounce back quickly.

PRACTICE

1. Next time you notice someone or something upsetting you, pause briefly, acknowledge your discomfort, and begin breathing through your nose slowly and intentionally. By extending your exhalations, you should feel calm within a few minutes.

2. When more than a few stressors pile up, you may need some movement to quiet your nerves. It is very difficult to think our way out of stress. Use your body instead. Here are a few possibilities:

    - Walk around the block.
    - Stretch your arms, legs, neck, and shoulders.
    - Dance to a favorite song.
    - Play a musical instrument or listen to music.
    - Vacuum your rugs, wipe down your countertops, or sweep the floor.

If we want to cultivate a sense of ease and calmness, there is no better way than to begin practicing mindfulness. Nurturing a nonjudgmental, present-moment awareness will boost our well-being and reduce feelings of anxiety and stress. Continue bringing your attention back to the present. How does mindfulness accomplish so much? Researchers have found it affects several areas. We become more skilled at regulating our attention; we increase our bodily and emotional awareness; and we change our self-perception.[39] Just like my interrupted bike ride, we notice how we are feeling and bring our attention back to this moment. Our bodies and minds don't take us on a ride we didn't sign up for.

DID YOU KNOW?

In parts of Africa, Australia, and the Pacific islands, native peoples practice "cradling," which helps to nurture their health and well-being. Cradling has four parts, and is practiced to connect with the good, the true, and the beautiful in one's nature.[40]

1. Lie on your back and place both hands over your heart.
2. Quietly acknowledge the qualities you appreciate about yourself.
3. Think about your strengths, the ways you contribute to others and your community, and the love you have offered and have received.
4. Take several minutes to allow your thoughts to sink into your mind and body.

Hopefully, you feel nourished, strengthened and ready to tackle your day.

I made the grave mistake of trying to shop at a local big-box store on the Saturday of college move-in. Cars were circling the completely full parking lot to find an open spot That scene should have been my cue to turn around and head home. But no, my innate optimism kept me on task. Luckily, I located a space at the back of the lot, parked, and strolled into the store. My first stop was the $3 bin section, selecting treats for my grandchildren, who were arriving at "Camp Kernion" the next day. Navigating the aisles was an exercise in precision driving, as they were overflowing with students and parents stocking up on dorm and apartment supplies. Movement was at a snail's pace, with many shelves completely bare. I managed to make my way through the shopping-cart traffic and found most of the items on my list, sometimes snagging the very last bottle of household supplies on the shelf.

After an hour of shopping for only ten items, my last stop was the candy aisle, which was again jammed with carts. I made the fateful decision to leave my cart at the end of the aisle and hustled to locate Pez candies and Jelly Bellies for the grandkids. Finding them after a sixty-second search, I returned to the spot I'd left my cart, and it was gone. My first thought was, "Did I leave the cart somewhere else?" I wandered around the adjacent aisles, peering into strangers' carts to see if someone had mistakenly taken mine. I searched for ten minutes, expanding my search area several aisles in each direction, but to no avail. I desperately queried a store worker about my missing cart, immediately realizing that was a silly question to ask. Resigned to the fact that my cart was lost, I walked to the front of the store to get another cart and begin my scavenger hunt again, only to find the cart area empty. I then scanned the checkout lanes and saw that the lines stretched through the aisles with more than twenty customers in each. No more shopping for me. I walked out of the store empty-handed.

What to do with my emotions? Of course I was very frustrated and bewildered. Even so, my first thought was that I had a good story to tell! My second thought was to acknowledge that if this was the worst thing that happened to me this week, I could consider it a great week. I walked across the long parking lot to my car, laughing to myself and thinking about how I would share this crazy experience with my friends.

The moral of the story? There are several here, but my first takeaway is this: Stuff happens. Let it go. If I carry this frustration around with me all day, the experience will dominate my emotions instead of allowing me to happily anticipate the arrival of my grandchildren. It's a simple choice we can make: Lug those disappointments around like a ten-pound sack of potatoes or drop the sack at your feet and find a silver lining in the experience.

Stress armor is all about how we can cultivate resilience. Several evidence-based practices that can help include:

1. The art of practicing gratitude, because the more we look for the positives in our lives, the more we see them and acknowledge them.

2. Nurturing your relationships, because friends and family can encourage us when we are faced with challenges and obstacles.

3. Getting exercise, for numerous reasons. Exercise helps us manage stress, produces endorphins, (a feel-good hormone that helps relieve pain), and promotes overall well-being. Since moving our bodies is so helpful to our mental health, aim for 150 minutes per week.

4. Practicing mindfulness, pausing every so often to take a few deep breaths. Or sitting for thirteen minutes in meditation. Yoga, tai chi, and slow walks are just a few practices that can reduce stress and boost our self-awareness.

5. Setting goals and problem-solving by focusing on what you can accomplish, then breaking the task into small steps. Look to people and other resources for assistance if you are facing a new challenge. Then pat yourself on the back each time you make good progress toward your goal.

6. Practicing self-compassion and self-care, prioritizing habits that nurture your overall well-being. These habits include getting good sleep, eating a balanced diet, engaging in a hobby, and embracing learning opportunities.

7. Cultivating meaning and purpose, because joining activities and groups that align with your values and vision for the world help you have a growth mindset.

In the end, you are the only one who can decide which of these strategies will work best for you. But your resilience muscles can be built with practice, allowing you to navigate life's challenges with greater ease.

WORRY AND OVERLOAD

It is during our darkest moments that we must focus to see the light.

—Aristotle Onassis

I met a woman at a conference in San Jose, California. Kathy shared a spiritual practice she's incorporated into her daily life for several years now. At the beginning of each year, she chooses one word that will guide her actions for the next twelve months: *patience*, *mercy*, *gratitude*, or *kindness*. Kathy begins each morning with the intention of embodying that word in all she does that day. She admitted it wasn't always easy to act on her chosen word, like when she was caught in a traffic jam and her word that year was *patience*. But she has found that this guiding practice has brought more meaning and purpose to her everyday life.

Worrying is like paying a debt you don't owe.

—Mark Twain

My mom worried about everything. She was the oldest daughter in a family of six children, and her father died when she was sixteen.[41] Consequently, Mom took on some of the wage-earning responsibilities and found an after-school job ironing clothes for twenty-five cents per shirt. Although I had a lot of practice, I never mastered the art of ironing a collared shirt. (But boy, could I get every last wrinkle out of a handkerchief or pillowcase!) Mom's life experience contributed to her sense of obligation to others, and she silently carried the mental burdens of family members. She was a good example of the adage, "Worrying is like a rocking chair: It gives you something to do, but it gets you nowhere." I somehow internalized that message early in life, probably as a result of watching my mom suffer needlessly.

When we spend our entire day worrying about everything, we damage our long-term physical, mental, and cognitive health.[42] One recommended strategy to manage stress and anxiety is to schedule concentrated worry time (but never before bedtime). You might choose to gather your concerns for several minutes after waking to get your worrying out of the way.

> *If in our daily life we can smile, if we can be peaceful and happy, not only we, but everyone will profit from it. This is the most basic kind of peace work.*
>
> —Thich Nhat Hanh

If you're fretting about issues in several categories like health problems, family issues, or financial stresses, you might want to set aside fifteen minutes for each concern. Or, limit your total worry time to half an hour each day. Begin by listing specific worries and steps you can take to deal with them. The goal is to sit and work through anxieties for this fixed amount of time. Eventually, with practice, we condition ourselves to let those anxieties go, or at least keep them at bay until the next scheduled worry time. That way, we aren't carrying them around with us. All. Day. Long. Our brains, bodies, and minds will be much healthier.

> *Welcome the present moment as if you had invited it. Why? Because it is all we ever have.*
>
> —Pema Chödrön

One of the most insidious features of stress is that it is contagious. Our experience of others, and their experience of us, will tune and prune the neurons of our brains. Every day, microscopic parts of our brains are changing as we interact with people. When we are in a stressful situation and are anxious, nervous, or overwhelmed, we will affect the people around us. Our worried facial expressions, nonverbal cues, and observable actions can bother and even upset others. I'm awestruck by this, and also dismayed! Our stress, then, is changing the brains and bodies of everyone we engage with. Yikes. I need to think about that the next time I am faced with a stressful situation. Remaining calm will help not only my heart and brain and health, but the hearts, brains, and health of all the people around me.

> *Over time, anything that contributes to chronic stress can gradually eat away at your brain—this includes verbal aggression, social rejection, severe neglect, and the countless other creative ways we social animals torment one another.*
>
> —Lisa Feldman Barrett

PRACTICE

This week, notice when you are feeling distressed or uneasy, and remember that your actions are affecting others. Taking a few deep inhalations and long exhalations, walking around your neighborhood, or doing a few stretches will not only soothe your nervous system, but will calm people around you, too.

GRATITUDE

Normal day, let me be aware of the treasure you are. Let me learn from you, savor you, bless you before you depart. Let me not pass you by in quest of some rare and perfect tomorrow.

—Mary Jean Irion

With each passing year, I become more aware of the everyday gifts of ordinary life. Perhaps this awareness comes from watching grandchildren discover puddles and leaves and rainbows and snowflakes. Or maybe I'm noticing the number of sympathy cards I now send—to friends who have lost parents as well as to people who, tragically, have lost children. It seems I'm constantly reminded that every single day is a gift.

Brother David Steindl-Rast, often called the "grandfather of gratitude," is an author and Benedictine monk. He is known and loved all over the world for his message that gratitude is the true source of happiness. He says, "We can be grateful *in* situations, if not *for* situations." Even when life is really, really hard, we can find something to be grateful for. And boy, do I know that's not easy. But here we are: Breathing. Walking. Seeing. Loving. Talking. Listening. The only appropriate response to this existence is simply *gratefulness.*

After an outdoor yoga class one Saturday morning during COVID-19, all of us yoga friends celebrated a classmate's seventieth birthday with watermelon, cupcakes, and mimosas. It was a time to be grateful for the 25,568 days Donna has been alive to enjoy family and friends, while being fully aware of the pain and challenges that have accompanied some of those days. As I acknowledged in my toast, to be human means to court sadness as well as joy, but we rejoice in the gifts of a new day and in the light that Donna brings to our lives. It was a simple commemoration celebrated six feet apart. We were happy to be together, even if the new "together" meant keeping our distance. We didn't take any aspect of our modest party for granted, as we might have done a few months beforehand.

The events of our world today may lean toward brokenness, but the practice of gratitude has the power to heal, to bring hope and energy to our lives. Gratitude is what boosts my spirit when the world starts to overwhelm me. We can pay attention to the good that surrounds us even as we acknowledge the difficulties. Finding small things to be grateful for can keep us energized in our efforts to make the world more just and equitable for all.

PRACTICE

Jot down three things you are grateful for, or send a thank you note to someone who deserves it. For example, I sent a note of appreciation to the elected official who provided improvement updates at our neighborhood meeting. I figured that he rarely gets a handwritten note of thanks. Research shows that writing a gratitude letter like this promotes the happiness and well-being of both sender and receiver. I feel happier just picturing him reading my note!

> *In normal life we hardly realize how much more we receive than we give, and life cannot be rich without such gratitude. It is so easy to overestimate the importance of our own achievements compared with what we owe to the help of others.*
>
> —Dietrich Bonhoeffer

Two gratitude exercises have been shown to be very effective in improving our well-being. The first is to recall when someone was genuinely thankful for something you did, or when you witnessed someone else receiving help that they were grateful for. Think deeply about the experience. How did you or someone else help? How did that impact you emotionally? Practice this for one minute, one to three times per week. Studies show that when we do this, our heart rates slow down, we experience joy and awe, and our fear and anxiety circuits are less active. In addition, the neural circuits for motivation and well-being increase, and we are more empathic.

The second gratitude exercise is to, at bedtime, write down three things that went well that day, no matter how small, and be specific. Instead of writing "A friend complimented me," write, "Sally told me how much she appreciated the reflection I read after class." Include why the positive event happened, how you felt in the moment, and how you feel recalling it. Do this once a week or more, and you will be creating new neural pathways that will attune your attention to the positive. Your stress will lessen, your sense of connection with others will grow, and your mental health will be strengthened.

These exercises counteract our natural tendency to focus on the negative (an evolutionary bias) and help us appreciate the good events that happen in our lives. The more we look for them, the more we see them, increasing our life satisfaction and ability to fall asleep. By savoring positive experiences, we extend their effects and boost their impact. Try this and see if it helps you as it has helped me!

I find it absolutely amazing that being thankful can change our brains and bodies by boosting our happiness and immune systems, and increasing our energy and generating calmness. Research shows that gratitude practices cause our brains to release dopamine and serotonin, the two most important neurotransmitters responsible for feel-good emotions. By practicing gratefulness every day, we can strengthen these neural pathways, creating long-lasting positive changes to our overall well-being.

> *A miracle happened: Another day of life.*
>
> —Paulo Coelho

DID YOU KNOW?

Grateful brains exhibit more activity in two regions: the anterior cingulate cortex (ACC) and the medial prefrontal cortex (mPFC), areas associated with our emotional processing, how we bond with other people and enjoy those interactions, our moral judgments, and our capacity to understand others and have empathy.

University of California Los Angeles (UCLA) Mindful Awareness Research Center (MARC) found that regularly expressing gratitude changes the molecular structure of the brain, keeping gray matter functioning and making us healthier and happier. Individuals who practiced gratitude for just eight weeks strengthened the areas of their brains associated with social cues, empathy, and reward processing.[43] Just eight weeks! Think of how much your brains will change and improve if you make gratitude a lifelong habit. You'll find more joy and enhance your connections to everyone around you.[44]

I contracted COVID-19 in March 2020. The illness was unlike any I've experienced: fever for eleven days, exhaustion for two months, and complete loss of taste and smell that only fully returned twenty months later. I learned a lot in the weeks it took to recover and in the months after my recovery. One lesson I hope to never forget was an all-encompassing *attitude of gratitude*. I'm grateful that I survived. I'm grateful that I've returned to my pre-COVID healthy self. It could have been much worse. I am thankful for every hug from a friend, every meal shared, every sunrise and sunset.

> *If you are grateful for your life. . . then you have to be grateful for all of it. You can't pick and choose what you're grateful for. It's a gift to exist, and with existence comes suffering.*
>
> —Stephen Colbert

I find it ironic that a common feature of our human lives is that we often count our blessings after challenging episodes, like my experience with COVID-19. A less dramatic gratitude opportunity happened when I was looking forward to a long walk in the woods one day. I changed into my hiking clothes, walked to my car, opened the door, sat down, and pressed the start button. Nothing happened. I tried it a second and third time. It still wouldn't start. I sat there for a moment, took a deep breath, and thought well, I'll call my husband, who had left just a few minutes ago. Jack could come back and take me to the trailhead, and I could still go for my walk.

As I waited for him, I began tallying all the things I was grateful for in that moment. First, I was grateful for Jack, who was happy to swing back home and play chauffeur. Second, I was grateful for the American Automobile Association, known as AAA, who would come and jump the battery. I was also grateful for neighbors who would lend us jumper cables. In fact, I saw our next-door neighbor on the trails, who offered his cables even before I asked. And I'm grateful for cell phones that enable us to communicate at the touch of a button whenever a need arises.

Why is it that we often need things to go wrong in order to remember to be grateful for what we have? Since my bout with COVID-19, every time I step onto a trail, even in freezing temperatures with three layers of fabric covering my mouth, I breathe in deeply and say a prayer of gratitude for the fragrant, earthy scents surrounding me. It was a great sadness during my recovery from COVID that I was unable to distinguish those scents. I feared that I would never again be able to enjoy them. After months of waiting and wondering, the first time I breathed in and detected the fragrance of honeysuckle, I was overcome. I stopped in my tracks and bent over, tears running down my cheeks as I sobbed uncontrollably with gratefulness. As long as I live, I will never, ever, take that aroma, or any other scent, for granted.

> *We can learn to rejoice in even the smallest blessings our life holds. It is easy to miss our own good fortune; often happiness comes in ways we don't even notice.*
>
> —Pema Chödrön

You might be wondering what happened to Jack and me after that fateful day in early March 1981 when we told each other we loved each other. I returned to St. Louis and, several nights later, fainted in my parents' kitchen. I was admitted to Mercy Hospital and diagnosed with toxic shock syndrome and severe anemia. I spent the next two months in bed recuperating, adding a third infection (mononucleosis) for good measure. Perhaps the profound uncertainty I was experiencing was partially to blame for contracting this last disease. What should I do? Continue with my plans to serve with the Maryknoll Sisters in Chile, or stay in the U.S. with Jack and begin our life together?

To gain some unbiased guidance, I visited a priest friend of mine, Fr. Gary Braun. After listening to my dilemma, he simply said, "Anne, God wants you to be happy. You will find a way to serve if you decide to stay here with Jack." It was some of the best advice I would ever receive. I canceled my plans to move to Chile and we were married the following February. My friend Mary flew back from South America to attend. Sixteen of our folk group friends from college were there, too. They drove from Pennsylvania to St. Louis and slept that weekend on the floor of my parents' house. They were there because they believed in us. We were thrilled to be surrounded by our good friends who had seen our love develop from the very beginning.

> *There is no surprise more magical than the surprise of being loved.*
>
> —Charles Langbridge Morgan

PRACTICE

Take a moment now to ponder a few of your beliefs, both important and trivial. Ask yourself these questions:

1. How do your beliefs impact your life?
2. Regarding the beliefs that guide your daily life, are you open to information that would alter them?
3. Do you actively question the quality and sources of information that you receive?

If there is just one idea to take away from this section, it is that our beliefs shape everything we are—physically, mentally, emotionally. They affect our bodies: how we move through the world, maintain our health, heal our aches and pains. They shape our thoughts, our goals, what we expect, what we attend to, and how we understand the world around us. And beliefs create the feelings we experience in response to life events. Are we happy and grateful, sad and frustrated, or scared or excited about the future? What we believe affects everything. So take time to review your beliefs and how they are influencing your life, for they are powerful forces.

PART II

BODIES

BREATHING TECHNIQUES

Only in the oasis of silence can we drink deeply from our inner cup of wisdom.

—Sue Patton Thoele

We hear steady streams of advice on how to keep our bodies healthy and strong. So you might wonder what more you could possibly learn about nurturing your bodily health. Well, as it turns out, there's quite a lot of new information that can help us maintain our physical well-being. And as a bonus, these practices also boost our mental health. Let's take an exploratory walk through some of the latest health practices. But keep in mind, we can't successfully adopt more than one or two new habits at a time.

When our grandson Percy was a baby, he struggled to pronounce "Gramma," and somehow settled on calling me "Nu-ma." Percy is now eleven years old, and the name has stuck. His two younger sisters also call me Numa, which I absolutely love. Why? Because when the word is spelled like it was by the ancient Greeks, *pneuma*, it means "spirit," "soul," or the "breath" of a person. So when I hear these sweet voices call for me, the rich meanings of my nickname bring a smile to my face, and I'm grateful for the gift of this accidental moniker.

Breath is central to our existence. Each one of us takes, on average, 22,000 breaths each day. That's a whole lot of inhaling and exhaling. When we consciously breathe, we pause and connect with the Source of Life, inviting us to inner peace and calm. Setting aside a few moments of silent breathing each day allows us to, as Sue Patton Thoele observes, draw from our inner wisdom that is waiting to be tapped.

We recognize that this connection between breath and spirit is found in a variety of cultures and religious traditions. Many Native American cultures teach that the breath represents the most tangible expression of the spirit in all living things. An example of one Native prayer that honors the breath is: "Oh, Great Spirit, whose voice I hear in the winds and whose breath gives life to all the world, hear me! I need your strength and wisdom." Likewise in the Hebrew tradition, *ruach* is translated "wind," "breath," or "spirit." In the book of Genesis, we see the phrase "breath of life" (2:7). In Sanskrit (and Hindi), the noun for "breath" (*prāṇa*) also carries the meaning of "life," "spirit," or "soul." So when we focus on our breath and breathe with intention, we nourish our bodies *and* our spirits.

Slow breathing is found in prayer practices around the world, and I've been surprised by the similarities in breath counts. From Buddhist monks to Jain adherents and many others, the chant of *Om*, considered by some the sacred sound of the universe, takes about six seconds to sing and another six seconds to pause and inhale between phrases. Researchers in Italy studied Catholics who were praying the Latin version of the rosary and found that the subjects' breathing patterns slowed to about five and a half breaths per minute while they prayed. The blood flow to their brains and their heart rate variability increased, in addition to other benefits.[45] These physical feelings of well-being associated with praying the rosary may be a factor helping to account for the continued popularity of this Catholic prayer practice.

Scientists have discovered that the optimum number of breaths per minute seems to be just six, and these traditional practices provide that number almost perfectly. I find this astonishing! We find that people all over the world from a wide range of spiritual practices slow their breaths similarly. There is ancient wisdom being passed along, as we see in these practices that there is more truth to the saying "prayer heals" than we ever suspected.[46]

Most people breathe too quickly and shallowly, which means that they aren't drawing in the optimal amount of oxygen with each breath. This rapid breathing ramps up activity in our amygdala, causing feelings of anxiety, anger, or fear to rise. Being more attuned to fear, we take in less oxygen with each breath. Neuropsychologists notice that people suffering from anxiety usually have high respiration rates. Quick breathing increases the activity in the amygdala, sending the body into a stressed state. In fact, if you want to work yourself into a frenzy (I know, who wants to deliberately do *that*?), simply start breathing rapidly for a minute. Most of us, of course, want the opposite outcome. By breathing slowly and deeply, we can usually quell our anxiety and fear, and our bodies will relax.[47]

> *Be kind to your sleeping heart. Take it out into the vast fields of Light and let it breathe.*
>
> —Hafiz

PRACTICE

Sit up tall, close your eyes, and take a few minutes to draw in some slow, deep breaths. Try to let go of any thoughts that pop up, as they most certainly will. Just relax and breathe.

Taking long, deep breaths enable our lungs to soak up more oxygen in fewer inhalations. How? A greater number of our alveoli, the tiny air sacs in our lungs, get inflated. We have about 300 million alveoli in our lungs, which would cover an entire tennis court if laid out flat. (Amazing!) Another interesting fact is that when we inhale, we are far better at learning new information than when we exhale—but of course we can't just inhale all the time without expelling the carbon dioxide building up in our bloodstreams. If we extend our exhalations, however, research shows that our heart rate will slow, and we will enjoy a sense of calm. These longer exhalations activate the "rest and digest" system in our bodies, washing away tension and anxiety. In addition, blood pressure lowers, the release of cortisol slows, and endorphins are released, helping to relieve pain and elevate our moods.

Practicing these slow, expansive breaths will benefit our bodies in many ways, including strengthening overall lung function. When we expand our lungs fully and deeply, our respiration rate slows, and the oxygen–carbon dioxide exchange is enhanced. If we regularly work on our breathing mechanics, they will improve, and in time the "work" of breathing correctly will lessen. Each of these outcomes boosts lung function, which is a long-term predictor of overall health, mortality risk, and longevity. Our lung fitness is closely connected to our general physiological health and aging processes, so practicing any of the breathing techniques below can be quite impactful. Just choose one or two you enjoy most![48]

Several breathing techniques have been found to reduce stress and anxiety. These include but are not limited to: rhythmic breathing, slow breathing, deep breathing, box breathing, prolonged exhales, brief breath-holds, cyclic breathing, and diaphragmatic breathing.[49]

Try This | 4-7-8 Breath

This is a very simple exercise that is used to reduce anxiety and aid in falling asleep:

1. Breathe in quietly through your nostrils for four (4) seconds.
2. Hold your breath for seven (7) seconds.
3. Then exhale through your mouth to the count of eight (8) seconds.
4. Repeat this sequence four times.

If you find the breaths and holds are too long for you, simply count faster or reduce the counts to half as long: a two-second inhalation, a three-and-a-half-second hold, then a four-second exhalation.

The first time I visited a doctor after recovering from COVID-19, I was a bit nervous. I'd never been anxious about medical appointments, even when I'd had some serious illnesses in the past. But due to the unknown nature of COVID-19 and its potential for long-lasting side effects, I began experiencing nervousness as I waited in various examining rooms. Consequently, my blood pressure readings were much higher than the readings I took at home. So I searched for effective ways to control my "white coat syndrome." I found a simple breathing technique to address the issue: the "physiological sigh." This breathing technique is the easiest and most efficient way to quickly reduce stress. What does it entail?[50]

> *Nothing begets wholeness in life better than a heartfelt sigh.*
>
> —Rabbi Nachman of Breslov

Try this | Physiological Sigh: Inhale, Inhale, Exhale

1. Stand or sit in a quiet area. Relax your body, particularly your jaws, neck, and shoulders.

2. Inhale slowly and deeply through your nose and notice your abdomen expanding.

3. Now quickly inhale through your nose and expand your chest fully, completely filling your lungs. Hold this breath for a moment.

4. Exhale slowly and gently through your mouth, completely emptying your lungs. This exhalation should last about twice as long as the combined inhales.

Repeat this cycle of breathing three times or more. When you are finished, sit for a few moments and note how you feel. Perhaps you are more relaxed, calm, and at ease in mind and body? Hopefully you can carry this feeling with you as you resume your daily routine.

> *When I hear somebody sigh, 'Life is hard,' I am always tempted to ask, 'Compared to what?'*
>
> —Sydney J. Harris

Try this | Box Breathing

Box, or square, breathing has been shown to reduce stress, manage pain, lower blood pressure, and improve focus. To practice this technique, sit up tall with your feet on the floor. Close your eyes and, if possible, breathe through your nose. Although four-second counts are typical, you can just as well use a three-second or five-second count.

1. Inhale for four seconds.
2. Hold your breath for four seconds.
3. Exhale for four seconds.
4. Hold for four seconds.
5. Repeat.

These practices show that we can use our breath to regulate our responses to stress, and this ability alone will improve our health in several ways.[51]

Nasal breathing is quite superior to mouth breathing. Why? Because mouth breathing changes our bodies and air passages in several ways, and all for the worse.

DID YOU KNOW?[52]

1. Mouth breathing decreases pressure in our upper airways and lungs, loosening the tissues in the back of the mouth. This results in less space for breathing. But these same tissues get a workout with nasal breathing, so the airways stay open and wide.

2. The oxygen delivered to the prefrontal cortex is disrupted. This is a crucial area of the brain associated with logical thinking, executive planning, and judgment.[53] Issues with concentration and memory can also occur.

3. Mouth breathing results in misaligned jaws, overbites, and underbites. The crowded mouth lacks the space for teeth to come in straight, so often produces crooked teeth.

4. Shallow or rapid breathing can cause poor oxygenation of the blood, which can negatively affect organs and other tissues.

5. Fast and shallow breaths contribute to stress, anxiety, and panic attacks.

6. Chest breathing and shallow breathing can cause tension in the neck, shoulders, and upper back muscles, leading to pain and discomfort.

7. Shallow breathing can affect the diaphragm's movement, which can lead to digestive problems such as bloating, constipation, and acid reflux.

The air entering our nostrils is better for our bodies because the nose filters heat and moistens the air for easier absorption in the lungs. Consequently, we are able to extract about 18% more oxygen with each breath if we breathe through our noses.[54] Since discovering these facts, I've begun breathing through my nose as much as possible, even during challenging bike rides when I'm huffing and puffing. But it's a simple way to help maintain my physical and cognitive health. It's certainly worth the effort, even if it only helps a little bit.

Interestingly, some research claims that breathing through the right nostril activates the sympathetic nervous system, increasing heart rate and blood pressure, while feeding more blood to the prefrontal cortex. Likewise, a few studies have argued that some connection can be shown with left nostril breathing and the parasympathetic system, lowering blood pressure, reducing anxiety, and cooling the body. But robust scientific research has not found strong evidence of these assertions due to small sample sizes and modest effects. More studies are warranted to fully understand and validate these claims.[55]

> *That moment of inward breath, that pause and awareness of 'how beautiful this is' is a prayer of appreciation, a moment of gratitude in which I behold beauty and am one with it.*
>
> —Jean Shinoda Bolen

As we have seen, the breath is one of the simplest yet most powerful instruments for cultivating overall well-being. When we consciously weave moments of breath awareness throughout our days, we open doorways to calm, create space for gratitude to flourish, nurture the conditions for joy to arise, and experience a deep integration of mind, body, and spirit. Consider this your invitation to begin this practice of presence today, not as another daily chore, but as a return to your body's natural wisdom.

PAIN

Pain is inevitable. Suffering is optional.

—Haruki Murakami

We might find ourselves breathing quickly or irregularly when we experience pain. And indeed, physical pain is inevitable, from skinning our knees as children to the accumulated bumps and bruises and assorted pains accompanying us as we make our way through life. But we can minimize our sensitivity to pain if we learn to deal with it skillfully. The Buddhist parable of the two arrows is instructive: It teaches that yes, pain happens. That's the first arrow. The second arrow is our response to the first, and that response is optional. If anguish, rumination, or distress accompanies the first arrow, we will augment the pain unnecessarily and experience the pain even more deeply. If we learn to accept the pain and not react to it, our suffering is minimized.

Medical professionals agree that evaluating and treating pain is a very difficult task. This is due to several factors. First, pain is highly subjective and difficult to assess with any accuracy. It is not just a bodily reaction, but stems from our brains, as well. Second, our psychological state—happy, sad, depressed, or energized—will influence our experience of it. Third, what we've been taught about pain via cultural beliefs and attitudes may also play a role in how pain is experienced. And finally, we may be experiencing pain from more than one source.

How can we lessen our reactivity to pain without medication? Several techniques are effective. These include listening to music, turning attention away from pain, and meditation. The last one, meditation, seems to change the way our bodies and brains process and respond to pain signals.[56] A consistent meditation practice can reduce activity in a few areas of the brain associated with pain perception and expand neural connectivity in others. Meditators increase their acceptance of pain and reduce their feelings of unpleasantness. Practitioners learn that the experience of pain is simply a mental event. The more I practice, the easier it is, so I apply this technique during colonoscopies, which I undergo without anesthesia. I simply note the discomfort without dwelling on it, chat with the doctor, and focus my eyes on the screen above as the camera moves through my body. It's amazing that we have this technology that allows us to see the inside of our bodies! Colonoscopies are an awe-inducing experience for me, as I view the walls of my colon and other internal organs.

Rachel Zoffness, PhD, a professor at the University of California San Francisco School of Medicine and specialist in the treatment of pain and pain management, has discovered that pain occurs due to the interplay of biological, psychological, and social components. Her research shows that patients will have better lives if they understand the mechanisms behind pain and take action to minimize its effect on them.[57] Since so many people suffer from chronic pain, Dr. Zoffness provides recommendations to help better manage the experience of pain.

TRY THIS

1. **Practice diaphragmatic breathing:** Take deep, slow breaths, engaging your diaphragm. Doing so can reduce your stress, help manage pain flare-ups, and boost relaxation.

2. **Do a body scan:** Starting at your feet, place your attention on each body part as you move up to your head. You'll find less tightness and tension, and a sense of overall calm.

3. **Be mindful:** Focus on being fully present and aware of your thoughts, feelings, and surroundings in a non-judgmental way. Cultivating an awareness of pain and emotion can reduce the discomfort and anguish associated with chronic pain.

4. **Restructure your thoughts:** Recognize when you have pessimistic thoughts about pain and replace them with more reasonable thoughts. Pain does not always mean damage.

5. **Pace yourself:** Break up your activities into small segments to avoid overdoing it, which can lead to pain flare-ups.

6. **Have fun:** Plan activities you enjoy to take your mind off your pain. Occasionally doing them with others is even better. You'll feel stronger both in body and spirit.

7. **Maintain good sleep habits:** Keep overhead lights dim until bedtime, sleep in a cool, dark room, and maintain a consistent sleep schedule.

8. **Plan for obstacles:** Look ahead to see where you might find roadblocks in your journey and develop strategies that will preserve your good habits.

Implementing a few of these strategies has helped me deal with some aches and pains quite effectively. Occasionally, my assorted joint injuries from overuse and normal wear and tear flare up. When the pain rises to a level that is higher than comfortable, I remember the advice in numbers 3 and 4 and try not to "awful-ize" my situation. I tell myself that the pain is not permanent and does not necessarily indicate damage. Scheduling a catch-up phone call with my sister or a good friend takes my mind off the pain. By redirecting my attention towards enjoyable activities, I calm my worries and forget about the discomfort.

> *Pain is our way of protecting us. Sometimes (the brain) is mistaken and the pain at that point is like a false alarm—meaning the alarm is going off but actually the body is healthy and sound.*
>
> —Yoni Ashar

Another pain researcher, psychotherapist Alan Gordon, has successfully developed an important approach to help patients dealing with chronic pain.[58]

DID YOU KNOW?

1. Realize the pain-brain connection: The chronic pain we experience is often caused by neural pathways in the brain rather than real tissue damage.

2. Pain is how our brain is trying to protect us. However, sometimes it is communicating pain when there is no concerning danger or damage.

3. Like Zoffness, Gordon notes that thoughts, emotions, and beliefs can influence our physical pain. He utilizes a psychosomatic technique that retrains the brain's response to pain. The person focuses on the pain without judgment, changing negative thoughts about the pain. This exposure therapy teaches the brain that there is no real danger.

4. Gordon also advises that we need to consider and deal with any emotions that might be contributing to a person's chronic pain.

Realizing that humans everywhere suffer with physical pain, we can be optimistic that these emerging insights into the nature of pain may offer relief for you or those you hold dear. Having witnessed the profound burden that persistent pain places upon those I cherish, I am genuinely hopeful that these new approaches might ease the daily struggles of all who grapple with pain.

MORNING LIGHT AND WALKS

Each day holds a surprise. But only if we expect it can we see, hear, or feel it when it comes to us.

—Henri Nouwen

A few years ago, I learned about the many benefits of exposing our eyes to natural light early in the morning. After discovering the amazing ways that morning walks can boost our well-being, I began incorporating them into my day.[59] So now the first thing I do most mornings, no matter the weather, is take a stroll for twenty to thirty minutes. As someone once said, "There is no inclement weather. There is just inappropriate clothing." (Although, after several days of subzero temperatures this past winter, I have to say that that weather qualified as "inclement.")

When sunlight reaches your eyes soon after you wake, it triggers a neural circuit that controls the timing of the hormones cortisol and melatonin, which affect sleep. Getting morning light prompts you to rise earlier the next day. It is also helpful to get some sunlight in the late afternoon or evening. Evening light has been shown to help anchor our internal clocks and encourages the correct level of melatonin, the sleep-inducing hormone.[60]

What are the benefits you can receive from your morning routine?

1. Morning sunlight sets your biological clock. When viewed for just two to ten minutes, sunlight has many positive health effects on the brain and other organs. The first, and perhaps the most important one for many of us, is that viewing morning natural light will help maintain proper circadian rhythms. Meaning we enjoy better sleep quality, better cognitive functioning, improved hormonal timing, and other benefits. So try to get outside within thirty to sixty minutes of waking.[61]

2. Your mood will improve and your cognitive abilities will be enhanced. Serotonin is a feel-good chemical, released when we are exposed to morning sunlight.

3. The pituitary gland releases a hormone that is activated by ultraviolet light, stimulating the desire to stop eating. This is why we tend to want to eat more in the wintertime. So getting a bit of sunlight on our eyes throughout the day helps to control our appetite.

One of my yoga students suffered from insomnia for years, trying every remedy imaginable. After learning about the benefits of morning walks, she began taking a morning stroll, and her sleep patterns are now vastly improved. Sometimes, but not always, the solution to our difficulties is a simple lifestyle tweak like this.

Other benefits to a morning walk include:

1. Optic flow occurs when objects in our vision field move in relationship to our bodies. This movement, particularly done in natural environments, quiets some circuits responsible for stress. Changes occur in brain activity and the nervous system, increasing relaxation. If you can't walk outside, moving around indoors also creates optic flow.[62]

2. The rhythmic nature of walking calms the mind and provides time for reflection and problem-solving.

3. Walking can also lower the risk for depression, resting heart rate, body fat, body mass index, and total cholesterol. Better yet, walk with friends.[63]

4. Panoramic viewing relaxes our eyes. We might try and spend ten minutes a day viewing objects off in the distance, at least half-a-mile away. This practice relaxes and flattens our lenses and reduces eye strain. That's why it's very calming to look at the horizon. Our eyes send signals deep into the brain stem, releasing stress.

TRY THIS

- On bright cloudless days, view the morning and afternoon sun for ten minutes. On cloudy days, which are more typical on my walks in Pennsylvania, aim for twenty minutes. If it's very overcast, shoot for thirty to sixty minutes.

- Don't wear a brimmed hat or sunglasses or hang out in the shade, as these will lessen the boost to your circadian clock.

- And never—never!—stare directly at the sun, as that can damage your eyes. Glasses or contacts will not compromise light strength, since they focus light into your neural networks.

- Don't forget to use sunscreen or wear clothing with UPF (Ultraviolet Protection Factor) fabric. As a former lifeguard whose skin protection was non-existent back then, I'm paying the price for the years I spent baking in the sun. No surprise that skin cancer has hit me twice already. So protect your skin and lips every time you head outdoors, no matter the time of day.

PRACTICE

Take a ten-minute walk each day this week as soon as you get out of bed. Set your clothes and shoes out the night before to minimize any friction in the morning. As you walk, practice noticing the fine details in objects you see along the way. Give thanks for several gifts in your life, which could be as minute as your morning cup of coffee or tea, or as meaningful as your family and friends. At week's end, see if you notice a difference in your sleep, your mood, your cognitive thinking skills, or your problem-solving.[64]

Whether you like staying up late at night or prefer greeting the rising sun, it's important to get some sunlight on your eyes as soon as possible after getting out of bed. And it should be outdoor light, which is *much* stronger than you'll get sitting by a window since glass filters out some ultraviolet light. Indoor light at a window on a sunny day will deliver up to fifty times less light intensity even when compared to outdoor light on an overcast day.

> *We were designed to get a lot of ultraviolet light on our eyes during the day and little during the night. The more of these cues to the time of day and night you can give your body, the better off you'll be.*
>
> —Dr. Andrew Huberman

Think that may be an exaggeration? So did I. I decided to test this myself, using the free app Light Meter to measure indoor versus outdoor light strength. On a sunny day, inside at the window, the highest reading I measured was 420 lux. Outside in the sunshine, the meter registered 55,000 lux. A huge difference! The experts were right.

You might wonder if you can simply turn on bright lights inside your home. It's better than darkness, but artificial lights don't emit nearly enough photons for the retina to signal your circadian clock.

> *Imagine that we could live each moment as a moment pregnant with new life. Imagine that we could live each day as a day full of promises.*
>
> —Henri Nouwen

Nouwen's observation is what I think about as I head out the door. What wonders will I see this morning? What gifts will be right in front of me, if I just open my eyes and ears? Looking at the sky, the clouds, the ground I walk on . . . listening to the wind in the trees, birds chirping. Being grateful for the gift of sight. And then taking in the scent of pine, fresh air, flowers, and honeysuckle in the spring or summer. Scents continue to be a blessing I richly appreciate, since I lost that for so many months due to COVID-19.

I pair my morning walks with my gratitude practice and meditative time. These early strolls have become a ritual for me as I set an intention for the day and expose my eyes to the sunlight. I begin the day thankful for life and the ability to walk, and I count my many blessings. The beauty of the natural world provides moments of awe as I look around and notice details on the dirt path. I see the various colors of leaves, watch squirrels scampering about, and hear the birds chirping from above. Every tree trunk is unique, as are the shapes of clouds above. So much to notice, see, and take in: simple, everyday beauty.

I return from the woods clear-minded, ready to focus on the day's tasks. Without this pause, I often feel unmoored, bouncing like a pinball from one thing to another, lacking the underlying calm and centered feeling that follows my walks. Of course, these strolls could easily take place on a city street or a suburban block, but I'm partial to the Pennsylvania woods near our home. It's a grounding practice I highly recommend for overall health and well-being.

> *Winter: quieting time to rest in the warmth of our heart's hearth . . .*
>
> —Nan Merrill

In the northern hemisphere, the darkest months of the year occur from November through February. Many of us struggle with the consequences of diminishing light, such as less energy and suppressed mood. When dark and cold days are ahead, we may need to turn our attention towards the quality of resilience: How can we keep our spirits and energy aloft as we journey forward? What steps can we take to nurture our spiritual, emotional, and physical well-being in the coming weeks and months? Here are two simple ways we can boost our resilience.

Try This

1. Take some deep breaths, lengthening your exhalations. Do this a few times every day. Exhaling longer than inhaling calms your nervous system. Perhaps sigh every once in a while. You can also place your attention on the sensations of breathing where you feel it most: chest, nose, throat, or lungs. Then take a moment to be grateful for this great gift of life.

2. Soothe your nervous system to encourage the release of oxytocin, a "feel good" hormone. How? Hug a family member, a pet, or even yourself, by crossing your arms over your heart. Be kind to someone, meditate, pray, schedule a Zoom call with an old friend, or tell someone you care about them. All of these can calm our nerves and boost our moods.

These exercises provide a pause in our days, feeding our spirits and resetting our emotional balance. They help us embody a little more presence and serenity.

If you have young children in your life, arrange for them to play outside for two hours each day to prevent nearsightedness. That occurs when the eyeball stretches and grows too long, causing distant objects to look blurry. But if we expose our eyes to natural light, it stimulates the release of dopamine, which can slow the eyeball from stretching.[65]

DID YOU KNOW?

Researchers have found that children who are outside for two hours each day have a significantly lower chance of developing myopia than kids who are inside most of the day.[66] Many hours spent on screens and digital devices can also contribute to eye elongation and myopia. Unfortunately, the number of children with myopia has increased at an alarming rate in the past few decades, due to surging screen time and decreased outdoor time.[67] In the U.S. alone, myopia rates have soared over the past fifty years, from 25% in 1971 to nearly 42% in 2017. Many of these cases are in children, who are becoming nearsighted at younger ages.[68]

Aren't you amazed by all the ways that light affects our bodies and spirits? The exquisite interplay between light and human health is quite remarkable, and, sadly, has been mostly overlooked. But now, armed with this knowledge, we can adapt our relationship with light, thereby elevating our vitality, mental clarity, and emotional resilience, improving our daily lives.

EXERCISE

Exercise is the closest thing we have to a miracle drug.

—Dr. Michael Joyner

If exercise were a pill, everyone would be taking it. The benefits are wide-ranging, long-lasting, and life-changing. That's not hyperbole. It's just the truth.

I'm lucky that I've enjoyed movement and exercise since I was a little girl. We had a gazillion kids in our new suburban neighborhood, and I loved running around our yard and neighborhood streets every day. Boys and girls of all ages were we, engaging in a wide range of activities: wiffle ball, freeze tag, hide-and-seek, roller skating, Ghost in the Graveyard, bike riding, army games, hot box and catch, swimming, running through sprinklers, and basketball. We would pause only to grab a glass of Kool-Aid and a bologna sandwich, and head back outside. I do remember whining to my parents about their insistence that I wear a shirt in hot weather. If the boys didn't have to, why should I? My five-year-old brain did not understand their logic ("Girls just have to wear shirts.") and I got really mad, yelling and stomping my feet. But Mom and Dad held firm about my clothing requirements, and eventually I gave up the fight. It wasn't the first time I argued about their restrictions simply because I was a girl and not a boy. My dad banned me from playing tackle football in our front yard when I was eight years old, worried the older boys would crush his skinny daughter. Again, I didn't understand it at the time, but I'm grateful now that none of my bones were ever broken. Wintertime provided cold weather activities like snowball fights, igloo building, and ice skating on a nearby pond or our backyard patio. I don't remember ever sitting in front of a TV during daylight hours, except throughout the summer of eighth grade, when we were spellbound watching the Watergate hearings.

Let's review the many ways exercise affects our brains and bodies.[69]

DID YOU KNOW?

1. Exercise decreases stress and produces less cortisol, so we feel calmer.
2. Exercise creates more robust immune systems.
3. Exercise lowers levels of inflammatory cytokines.
4. Exercise improves emotional processing and lessens social anxiety.
5. Exercise helps slow or prevent neurological conditions such as Parkinson's, Alzheimer's, and multiple sclerosis.
6. Exercise may provide euphoria, due to the production of endorphins, dopamine, anandamide (an endocannabinoid), and other neurochemicals.
7. Exercise increases energy, focus, and attention.
8. Exercise increases the neurotransmitters serotonin and norepinephrine, which accelerate information processing.
9. Exercise slows aging and buffers against premature telomere shortening due to extreme stress.[70]

10. Exercise improves memory and decreases brain fog.
11. Exercise improves blood circulation and increases our sensitivity to insulin, stabilizing blood sugar levels.
12. Exercise increases antioxidant production, so free radicals (which cause cellular damage and can lead to cancer and other diseases) are neutralized.
13. Exercise builds bone health.

And there's more.

Exercise spurs neurogenesis and neuroplasticity, creating new neurons and cells, as well as strengthening existing synapses. Brain-derived neurotrophic factor (BDNF) is the name of the molecule that helps the brain produce new neurons, or brain cells. Research shows that exercise significantly increases BDNF levels, but it must be moderate-to-intense aerobic exercise, or resistance training with moderate to heavy weights.[71] Aerobic exercises and resistance training also affect how genes are expressed, leading to changes in neuronal connections and functions, which are highly beneficial for cognitive functioning. The hippocampus, an area of the brain associated with learning and memory, can grow new connections when we exercise regularly. So our ability to remember information is boosted, whether we are in academic settings or just playing card games with family and friends.

Exercise also functions as a clean-up crew for our bodies. When we work up a sweat, our cells get to work, too, cleaning and recycling damaged particles so there's less "junk" buildup. Exercise prevents these damaged molecules from accumulating and contributing to inflammation and disease.

> *The only bad workout is the one that didn't happen.*
>
> —Anonymous

Moderate exercise also seems to have anti-inflammatory effects, regulating the immune system and excessive inflammation.[72] This is important, given the new insights neuroscience research is uncovering into the potential role of inflammation in anxiety and depression. There is also evidence of the positive effects of exercise on the neurotransmitters dopamine and endorphins, brain chemicals that send signals between neurons. Both of these are involved in positive mood and motivation. Importantly, research shows exercise can actually reduce depressive symptoms as effectively as psychotherapy, while providing mild to moderate relief from anxiety.[73]

A study from 2020 shows for the first time that low and high exercise intensities influence brain function differently.[74] Researchers discovered that low-intensity exercise triggers brain networks involved in cognition control and attention processing, while high-intensity exercise primarily activates networks involved in affective/emotion processing.

If you take a leisurely approach to your workouts, you'll be happy to know that a study from Norway found that people who performed harder workouts didn't live any longer, on average, when compared with people who did more moderate workouts.[75] Both groups had similar levels of cardiovascular disease and deaths from cancer, but people who performed more intense workouts had higher levels of physical fitness and certain measures of mental health.

At the end of my daily morning strolls, I usually spend a minute walking backward, mainly to take pressure off my knees on a steep decline. I check the asphalt carefully, and keep my eyes on the path as I head downhill. Only recently did I learn this practice has benefits for both brain and body. It strengthens our legs, builds coordination and balance, and even helps manage pain. Backward walking engages glutes, calves, shins, and muscles in the feet and ankles. I know from experience that it also reduces the force exerted on our knees and lower back.

But walking backward also provides cognitive benefits. Research shows that it can boost cognitive flexibility and executive functioning, while increasing spatial awareness and navigation skills. Scientists believe backward walking may also promote neuroplasticity through activation of brain areas associated with attention, motor planning, and visual-spatial processing.[76]

TRY THIS

Try walking backward a few minutes each day, with this caveat: Be careful! Before you begin, check your surroundings to avoid tripping and falling and winding up worse for the wear.

> *You don't have to go fast, you just have to go.*
>
> —Anonymous

One enjoyable way to get moving is to connect exercise with socializing, since both provide physical and mental health benefits. Our exercise buddies can help us stay motivated and on track. We can walk in nature or stroll around our neighborhood with others. I often take longer walks with my friends Colleen or Susy at a nearby county park. We share the latest family news and laughter, discuss the highs and lows of the week, and walk farther than if we were alone. The hour flies by, and my legs are tired but my spirits are lifted. However, I'm less likely to check in with how my body is feeling. On a subzero winter day, my fingers were nearly frostbitten. Susy and I walked and chatted and I hadn't noticed how cold my hands had become. I couldn't control my fingers for more than an hour afterwards, so I learned a good cold-weather lesson: Wear warmer gloves and occasionally check in with my extremities when I'm out in the bitter cold.

We might also consider taking a walk after a meal. A ten-minute walk, thirty to forty-five minutes after eating, will help regulate your blood glucose. Our glucose levels rise after eating, so taking a walk allows our muscles to use some of that glucose for energy. The movement also aids with insulin sensitivity and digestion, as the glucose is gradually released into the bloodstream instead of spiking.[77] If you prefer moving to music, start a dance party in your kitchen post-meal. Any gentle movement after a meal helps your cells use energy more efficiently and store less sugar as fat, and improves your heart function and overall health.

TRY THIS

After your next dinner, take a walk around your block, or even around the rooms of your home. Or if you prefer moving to music, put on a favorite song and dance away! Any post-dinner movement will be good for your body.

One form of exercise that is skyrocketing in popularity is pickleball. All racquet sports, including pickleball, develop hand-eye coordination, spatial awareness, reflexes, balance, cardiovascular health, and agility; and they help relieve stress. In addition, these games require strategic thinking and focus, while providing conversations with others. Amazingly, participating in racquet sports, including ping pong, can increase a lifespan by up to ten years.[78] So many benefits—and great fun—from one activity. No wonder millions of Americans have taken up pickleball!

Okay, so we know exercise is essential to our health and well-being. But you might have just one question: How much time do I need to spend exercising to derive these benefits?

The Department of Health and Human Services recommends 150 minutes (2.5 hours) of moderate-intensity aerobic activity or 75 minutes (1 hour and 15 minutes) of vigorous-intensity aerobic activity per week.[79] Or you can strive for an equivalent combination of moderate and vigorous activities. Some moderate forms of exercise include brisk walking, pickleball, yard work, and dancing. Intense exercise would include running, biking on hills, swimming laps, and stair climbing.

Adults are encouraged to engage in muscle-strengthening activities two to three days per week, using weights or resistance bands. These exercises help preserve muscle mass, boost metabolism, reduce the risk of injury, and improve bone density and mental health. Each workout should involve all of the major muscle groups using a variety of exercises. Every four to eight weeks, it is good to change up your routine to protect against overuse injuries and boredom. You can accomplish this by varying the weights, number of reps, order and types of exercise, or by using different equipment. By following these recommendations, you'll continue building or maintaining your muscle development and strength into your golden years. Interestingly, wall sits, which are often part of strength training, have been shown to be the best exercise to lower blood pressure.[80]

DID YOU KNOW?

Why is strength training so important? Because without it, after the age of thirty, we lose between three and five percent of muscle mass each decade. After fifty, we continue needing proper resistance training along with adequate protein intake to keep from losing one percent of muscle mass per year. But here's the good news: Strength training and proper nutrition can slow and even reverse some age-related muscle loss. It's also another avenue towards protecting your cognitive health.[81]

Before the pandemic, I attended weight-training classes at our local gym. Now, I use a set of hand weights at home and watch YouTube strength training videos, which run from thirty to sixty minutes. These provide a wide variety of classes and relieve the burden of planning workouts on my own. Some of my favorite videos are from Juice and Toya, Kaleigh Cohen, growingannanas, and HasFit.

Until recently, I thought a sauna was mostly used by health club members and professional athletes—that is, people who had the time and money to relax after intense exercise. And to be honest, my mental picture of a sauna user was a heavyset man surrounded by steam, a white towel draped across his shoulders. But in the past few years, I've been hearing more and more about sauna's wide-ranging benefits. It is now a fast-growing practice for several good reasons, all backed by scientific studies. So after reading about its advantages to overall health, my husband and I bought a sauna kit, and we built one in our basement. And when I say, "we built one," I mean Jack assembled it and I stood around admiring his work and occasionally holding a tool. It is a simple, one-person wooden box, and provides a relaxing, contemplative experience that I particularly enjoy after a long workday or exercise session.

What are the benefits of sauna?

1. **Improves cardiovascular health.** When we sit in a sauna, our heart rate increases and blood vessels widen, boosting blood circulation and improving heart function. This increased circulation eases muscle soreness, improves joint mobility, lowers blood pressure, and promotes relaxation.[82]

2. **Aids in the treatment of depression.** Sauna ultimately lowers body temperature. Researchers recently found a link between higher body temperatures and depression. Although it sounds counterintuitive, heat exposure causes cooling of our overall body temperatures.[83]

3. **Eliminates some toxins, though in limited quantities.** The liver and kidneys are much more effective at ridding the body of chemicals and toxins than sauna.

4. **Regulates sleep patterns with regular use, while also alleviating chronic pain.** It reduces stress levels and releases endorphins, a feel-good hormone. The term "endorphin" is derived from the words "endogenous morphine," indicating its benefits are analogous to the powerful drug morphine, without having any of its side effects.

5. **Improves brain function.** Since sauna use can increase circulation in the entire body, including the brain, it can aid in clearing brain fog and boosting cognitive performance. Frequent sauna use also predicted a decreased risk of dementia in Finnish bathers.[84]

Finland has a long history of sauna use, dating back some 2000 years. It is a deeply rooted cultural and social institution in this Nordic country of only 5.5 million citizens, as evidenced by the more than three million saunas found throughout the country in offices, public facilities, apartment buildings, and private homes. So it's natural that Finnish men were the subjects of a long-term study that found those who used saunas four to seven times a week were significantly healthier than men who used saunas just once a week. They had less incidence of cardiac disease and heart attacks, and had a 40 percent lower risk of all-cause mortality.[85] But scientists have not yet uncovered the mechanism for these benefits. Perhaps it is due to the hot room, or the relaxation time, or the camaraderie between the men, or a combination of all of these factors. Further studies are needed to discover exactly why sauna leads to better heart health and longevity. In the meantime, I'm heading downstairs to warm up, relax, and perhaps add a few minutes to my life.

Unless you've been hiding under a rock your entire life, you already knew that exercise is important for maintaining your health and well-being. But hopefully this chapter has added to your knowledge by providing additional insights and strategies that will fuel your desire to move your body daily. Becoming an ultramarathoner or a bodybuilder isn't required. But consistency is. We just need to get up and off our chairs and couches and move and groove as we are able. I promise you, the more you get moving, the better you'll feel.

YOGA

A relaxed body allows for a focused mind.

—Anonymous

Yoga is a gentle form of exercise with many of the same benefits as strength training. As a yoga teacher for over fifteen years, I've seen these benefits accrue in myself and in my students. In our weekly classes, we focus on the stretching, balance, and strength aspects of the exercises. These yoga poses help us maintain our physical health and flexibility, while providing an avenue for relaxation and stress reduction. At the end of each class, I share an inspirational message of gratitude, hope, kindness, or compassion. Moving our bodies together and supporting one another through the ups and downs of life, we've become an encouraging, caring community.

Here's a summary of how yoga nurtures our well-being:[86]

1. Brain cells develop new connections, improving cognitive skills like memory, attention, and learning. Our brains naturally shrink a bit as we age, particularly in the areas associated with memory and thinking. But scans show that practicing yoga regularly seems to preserve the size of key areas of the brain, providing protection against age-related diminishment in memory and other cognitive skills.[87]

2. Yoga maintains bone health—similar to strength training, but gentler. Holding poses creates muscle resistance that pulls on our bone attachments, strengthening the bone and thwarting advancement of osteoporosis. It also contributes to spinal health, as it helps to maintain our vertebrae and discs. A study by Columbia University researchers found that a twelve-minute yoga sequence, done frequently, contributed to bone mineral density improvements in the spine, hips, and femur.[88]

3. Yoga can be a sleep aid for people with full-fledged insomnia. People in one study fell asleep faster after eight weeks of yoga compared to people who received only sleep instructions. And the more you practice, the more your sleep will improve.

4. Research also shows that yoga may improve executive functions, such as reasoning, decision-making, learning, reaction time, and accuracy on tests of mental acuity.

5. Like all exercise, yoga is a mood booster. Since it focuses on slowing the breath during the poses, it also promotes a more relaxed state. Yoga lowers levels of stress hormones, increases the feel-good hormones like endorphins, and brings more oxygenated blood to your brain. It also increases brain chemicals that lift mood and decrease anxiety.

6. Yoga often lessens back pain, improves range of motion and flexibility, and enhances focus.

The American College of Physicians recommends yoga as a first-line treatment for chronic low back pain. In addition, when patients with knee osteoarthritis or rheumatoid arthritis practice yoga, they report less pain and improved overall symptoms.[89]

I hope all these remarkable, transformative benefits of exercise help motivate you to move a bit more each day, particularly if you haven't incorporated exercise into your days for a while. Exercise is a foundational habit that can transform a life, cultivate more joy, boost mental and cognitive health, and provide greater longevity.

TRY THIS

1. Find a yoga class near you, a video online, or check out a yoga video from your local library. If you're new to yoga, look for a beginner class. I provide a few yoga videos on my website, too, under the "More from Anne" tab at www.cardsbyanne.com.

2. If racquet sports are more your jam, look for an opportunity to play ping pong, pickleball, or tennis in your community.

DIET

If your great-grandmother wouldn't recognize it as food, maybe you shouldn't eat it.

—Anonymous

There's so much to say about diet, but we could pretty much sum it up as this: Eat like your great-grandmother probably did—whole foods, colorful fruits and veggies, lean protein, healthy fats, and little, if any, ultra-processed foods (UPFs for short). When you see an ingredient list with items you wouldn't find in your kitchen, it's best to leave it on the store shelf. We aren't going to review dietary guidelines here, as those can be found everywhere and cater to each individual's needs and taste buds. But we will take a quick look at UPFs, since more and more research is showing that UPFs contribute to an alarming number of health issues.

The British Medical Journal, one of the most respected medical resources in the world, recently published startling statistics directly linking ultra-processed foods to thirty-two adverse health outcomes. These include increased rates of Type 2 diabetes, obesity, hypertension, metabolic syndrome, some types of cancer, wheezing, anxiety, depression, dementia, sleep issues, and deaths from all causes.[90]

Harvard researcher Dr. Christopher Palmer has studied ultra-processed foods for many years and has seen how they contribute to the world's mental health crisis. His work emphasizes that UPFs severely disrupt metabolic health and harm our physical and mental health in a variety of ways.[91] How do they do that? These foods are mostly high in saturated fat, salt, and sugar, and they tend to squeeze out healthy ingredients needed in an optimal diet. Plant-based foods containing polyphenols are antioxidants and anti-inflammatory, so eating highly processed foods leaves less room for the good stuff in a diet containing fruits and vegetables.

Eating well is important for maintaining our mental health; the more we include fresh and minimally processed foods in our diets, the lower the risk for depression and anxiety. We require a diverse gut microbiome to maintain optimal physical and mental health. But several studies have shown that diets containing high levels of ultra-processed foods are associated with a less diverse gut microbiome.[92]

Manufacturers often add flavorings and emulsifiers for taste, as well as colorings and other cosmetic additives. By maximizing palatability and absorption, people can consume large amounts before feeling full. Unfortunately, these additives may disrupt the function of brain chemicals such as serotonin, norepinephrine, and dopamine, essential neurotransmitters for mental well-being. They are often engineered to be highly addictive—even as addicting as smoking.[93]

I hesitate to call most UPFs "food," since many contain little, if any, whole-food ingredients. In fact, when I'm in a grocery store with my grandchildren and they ask to buy a highly manufactured treat, I explain that it's not really food. And I try to avoid the chip and snack aisle altogether. These highly processed foods are more like a small dose of poison for their bodies and brains. If you'd like to know how to avoid these UPFs, I recommend you read "What's the Difference Between Processed and Ultra-Processed Food?," written by Sarah Garone, and published at healthline.com.[94] It is an excellent guide to help you select healthy foods on your next trip to the grocery store.

Another issue concerning junk food consumption is that diets high in sugar and fat may contribute to long-term memory issues in teenagers. Scientists conducted a study that found a diet high in ultra-processed foods created a gut environment that caused memory impairments. These cognitive declines continued even after switching to a healthier diet.[95]

A 2020 study from Stony Brook University revealed that brain changes associated with aging can be seen at a much younger age than would be expected, as early as the late forties. The study suggested that this process may be prevented or reversed with dietary changes that minimize the consumption of simple carbohydrates, like table sugar, white bread, pastries, and desserts. Some complex carbs you might want to add to your diet include oatmeal, brown rice, multigrain pastas and breads, and most fruits.[96] This dietary advice isn't necessarily new, but the consequences of a healthy diet are so remarkable, it bears emphasizing what you might already know.

TRY THIS

1. Add one colorful fruit, vegetable, or a different grain to your menu this week, one that you haven't eaten in a while.
2. Find a recipe and make a meal with a non-red meat base, like cod, salmon, beans, or tofu.

Since I am particularly interested in all the ways we can maintain our health as we age, I'll summarize the six most important steps to take to achieve that goal.

First, engage in resistance or strength training twice per week. A study in the American Journal of Medicine found that muscle mass is a better predictor of longevity than body mass index (BMI).[97]

Second, eat less meat, and choose the best quality you can afford—or, forgo meat entirely. Daily red meat consumption, particularly processed meats, is linked to a higher risk of death from cardiovascular disease and cancer.

Third, do something that makes you feel healthy every day. The healthier the subjects participating in studies felt, the longer they lived. (See the section on the "Placebo Effect.")

Fourth, exercise regularly, as exercise helps protect our brains from aging. Increased blood flow helps to grow new neurons, protect memory function, and maintain overall brain volume, which usually shrinks as we age. Exercise also protects against brain changes associated with dementia in people aged seventy-five and older. Starting at any age will provide benefits. Beginning an exercise program in middle age can prevent brain deterioration in older age. And don't stop! It takes only ten days of inactivity to see blood flow declines in exercisers' brains.

Fifth, aim for four servings a day of whole grains like barley, bulgur, quinoa, brown, red, black or wild rice, oatmeal, popcorn, whole-wheat flour, and whole-grain cereals, breads, and pastas. (I make a mean batch of popcorn almost daily, using a Nordic popper, Orville Redenbacher popcorn, and canola oil. Add a dash of salt and alternative butter. Yum!) Consume four servings of whole grains per day and you'll be 22 percent less likely to die prematurely than people who ate little or no whole grains.

And sixth, socialize! Make time for your friends, as they will affect the quality and length of your life. People who lack social ties and support have higher inflammation levels, higher blood pressure, and larger waistlines, according to the research. I just hosted a Zoom call with two old friends, one of whom we haven't seen in over forty years. Mary, Carl, and I had a great time catching up, and vowed to meet again soon to continue the fun. Due to the gift of online meeting options, we no longer need to live in the same area as our friends to share time together. Connect in any way you can, and your body, brain, and spirit will benefit.

Most of us care deeply about our brain health, and it turns out that there are several foods that boost brain health while also supporting our cardiovascular systems.[98] The first is dark leafy greens, which contain vital nutrients supporting brain health. Vegetables like spinach, kale, and broccoli may help maintain cognitive abilities as we age.

Secondly, we should try to eat fatty fish twice a week, as they are abundant in omega-3 fatty acids. These healthy fats are associated with reduced levels of beta-amyloid, a protein linked to Alzheimer's disease. Good choices include salmon, cod, canned light tuna, and pollack. Plant-based sources of omega-3s include flaxseeds, avocados, and walnuts.

Third up are flavonoids—compounds found in berries that provide their bright colors, but more importantly, help improve memory. Women who ate two or more servings of strawberries and blueberries each week delayed declines in memory for up to two-and-a-half years.

Fourth, my two favorite beverages after water: coffee and tea. These two drinks may also protect mental functioning due to their caffeine content. Higher caffeine intake seems to correlate with better cognitive performance, and may also solidify new memories.

And lastly, an extra word about walnuts! They are the best nuts for the brain and body. Walnuts provide protein and alpha-linolenic acid, an omega-3 fat linked to lower blood pressure and healthier arteries. Toss them in salads and oatmeal, or eat by the handful.

As we have seen, our food choices profoundly influence our physical capabilities, emotional health, and cognitive functions. The ability to express our unique talents and skills is dependent upon proper nutrition, as it provides greater stamina, sharper focus, and psychological steadiness—essential resources for working effectively and contributing meaningfully to our families and society. I am hopeful that you have been inspired to tweak your diet in one or more ways so that you might enjoy even more vibrant, productive days in the years ahead. Isn't that what each of us longs to experience?

SLEEP

And if tonight my soul may find her peace
in sleep, and sink in good oblivion,
and in the morning wake like a new-opened flower
then I have been dipped again in God, and new-created.

—D. H. Lawrence

A few summers ago, we moved to a townhome from our suburban house. We had accumulated too much stuff in twenty-four years, and it was a herculean task to decide what to keep, what to donate, and what to toss. My fragmented sleep indicated that all of those decisions were wearing on my mind. I thought that the physical labor involved in moving mountains of boxes would send my body into deep slumber, but I was wrong. The stressors associated with the move got the better of me. Thankfully, after the move-in weekend concluded, my sleep patterns returned to normal.

But to be honest, most of us experience disruptions to our sleep from time to time, and only one in three Americans report getting sufficient sleep on a regular basis. Let's first take a brief look at the types of sleep, then dive deeper into why our shut-eye time is so critical, and how to improve it.

There are two major types of sleep: REM (rapid eye movement) sleep, which we might refer to as "dreaming" sleep; and non-REM sleep, or quiet sleep. Both are important for our well-being but are different from each other in significant ways.[99] We begin the night with non-REM sleep, which has three stages as we gradually fall into deep sleep. During the last stage, growth hormone is released, helping the body repair and regrow tissues, build bone and muscle, and strengthen the immune system to fight infections.

REM sleep comes on the heels of non-REM sleep and is restorative, clearing out irrelevant information in our brains and boosting our abilities to learn and remember. Studies from Harvard Medical School and elsewhere show that people learn new tasks better after a night's sleep that includes REM sleep. When REM sleep is thwarted, that improved ability is lost. But if non-REM deep sleep is interrupted, these improvements are not affected. So it is vitally important as we age to get enough REM sleep to preserve our memory and cognitive functions.

Oftentimes, people believe that adults need less sleep as they age, but this is not true. Yes, older adults often find they sleep more lightly and get less deep sleep, but studies show that their sleep needs are the same as their younger counterparts.

A chronic lack of sleep is linked to many physiological and psychological problems, such as poor memory, mood disorders, obesity, cancer, lowered immunity, and disrupted blood sugar regulation. But there are a few simple ways to ensure a good night's sleep. Ditch the sleeping pills, for starters: They do not provide the restorative properties of natural sleep. And be careful with caffeine, as it can affect sleep for up to twelve hours, depending on your sensitivity. Same with alcohol, which will fragment your sleep and block your REM sleep.[100]

Another good piece of advice is to dim your lights after 10:00 p.m. You don't have to turn your house into a cave, but turn off bright overhead lights, or at least reduce their intensity. Choose amber light over blue light, and place lamps physically low in the room.

When you head to bed, keep your room dark. Why? Because our biological clocks are regulated by light exposure. The functioning of our metabolism, muscles, and brain are all dependent upon our circadian rhythms, and disruptions affect those functions. Numerous studies have shown that higher light exposure between the hours of 12:30 a.m. and 6:00 a.m. means a greater risk of developing Type 2 diabetes. Getting a good night's sleep is an important part of regulating blood glucose.[101]

Other researchers discovered a link between nighttime light and the risk for Alzheimer's disease, especially for people younger than sixty-five years old.[102] If you need a nightlight for your safety or comfort, keep the light as low to the ground as possible. Use one with warm light bulbs in the red/orange range, which are better than bright blue or white lights.

I hardly need to say this, but please avoid checking your phone in the middle of the night, since this light will communicate to your body that it is daytime. This interruption can alter your sleep for several days. It's like jet lag: If you're looking at your phone at 2:00 a.m., you might as well be in Dubai in the middle of the day.

Some people use weighted blankets to help them sleep better. If you want to try it, use a blanket equal to between five to twelve percent of your body weight. One study found using a twelve percent weighted blanket increased a participant's melatonin concentration in their saliva by about 30 percent. It's possible that the weight of the blankets induces deep relaxation, resulting in less awakenings and an easier time falling asleep.[103]

> *To sleep, perchance to dream.*
>
> —William Shakespeare

Chronic sleep deprivation also impacts highway safety. Approximately fifty million drivers are speeding along our roadways every month while struggling to stay awake, causing twenty percent of car crashes. We can understand why drowsy driving would cause accidents, but how does the lack of sleep cause so many health issues?

For one, sleep deprivation is associated with inflammation. We fight disease and injury with this immune response, but if inflammation runs unchecked throughout our bodies, a whole host of problems result. Scientists know that blood pressure drops when we sleep, and our blood vessels relax. But lack of sleep may truncate this decline, triggering cells to activate inflammation. In addition, our brains get a bit of housecleaning every night during sleep, as beta-amyloid proteins and other waste products linked to brain cell damage are swept away. If we sleep poorly, the cleaning is less thorough, like a housekeeper dusting your furniture but not vacuuming your rugs. This partial cleaning allows these proteins to build up (a potential precursor to Alzheimer's disease) and inflammation to develop. As they build up in the brain's frontal lobe, they begin to impair the deep sleep that is essential for memory consolidation. So quality sleep is essential for maintaining the brain's waste-clearing system and our cognitive abilities.[104]

Sleep apnea, where breathing repeatedly stops and starts, is another issue affecting our health. I am particularly interested in this topic, as it is prevalent in my family members. I overcame moderate sleep apnea for a few years by training myself to breathe through my nostrils and by sleeping on a wedge pillow. Unfortunately, the cure did not last, and I now use a CPAP (Continuous Positive Airway Pressure) machine, which medical professionals often recommend. When we suffer from frequent interruptions, we have a 420% greater risk of cardiovascular death. Why? Because when oxygen levels drop, these frequent pauses in breathing put extra stress on our hearts: Blood pressure rises, the heart beats irregularly, and stress hormones are released. Couple these unhealthy side effects with a higher likelihood of premature cognitive impairment, and sleep apnea is a condition not to be ignored.

An interesting Australian study found that impairments to the glymphatic system, which removes waste from the brain, were associated with the onset of ALS, also known as Lou Gehrig's disease.[105] The study authors also cited other human behaviors that seem to contribute to effective glymphatic clearance, including side sleeping. Yep, you heard right. Side sleeping! I was astounded when I read about that. How and why would that position clear out brain detritus better than others? Study author David Wright surmises that it might be related to "gravity, compression, and stretching of tissue." So if you don't sleep on your side, you might want to start doing so.

What to do if you find yourself awake and not able to go to sleep or return to sleep? Many experts recommend getting out of bed and going to another room. They tell us that if you hang around your bed wide awake, your brain will associate the bed with wakeful activity, thereby making it even harder to fall back to sleep. Grab a book (no screens!) and read in dim light until you're sleepy.

Alternatively, if you'd rather not head to another room, try prayer or meditation. It will calm your nervous system and provide other benefits, as well. I practice this every so often, grabbing my earbuds (so as not to disturb my husband) to listen to a 22-minute guided meditation.[106] I rarely hear the last half of the recording, since after ten minutes I'm usually fast asleep. You might want to try this the next time you're struggling with wakefulness in the middle of the night.

What if you had a terrible night's sleep and you want to "make up" for it? The bad news is that you can't. Sorry to say, your brain is not a bank that can store deposits and compensate for losses. Even after we've had a few nights of "catch-up sleep," we continue having deficits in memory. And unfortunately, we aren't good at judging just how much the sleep debt is affecting us.[107]

However, one activity can help our sleep-deprived bodies. If we experience just a few nights of shortened sleep, our bodies have decreased insulin sensitivity and are less able to regulate glucose. One study showed that four hours of sleep for just one night led to acute insulin resistance. But the good news is that a high-intensity interval workout was able to reverse some of those increases in blood glucose caused by lack of sleep.[108]

Sleep regularity is another good habit to maintain. Going to bed and waking up at consistent times is actually more important than how long you sleep, as long as mid-sleep interruptions are kept to a minimum. Sleeping six hours every night on a consistent schedule was associated with a lower risk of early death than sleeping eight hours with very irregular habits.[109]

Try This

If you have trouble falling asleep or staying asleep, try using a weighted blanket, or find a sleep-inducing meditation on the Insight Timer (free) or Calm (subscription) apps.

When we aren't getting enough restorative shut-eye, our brain registers that as a threat and alerts our body that we are starving. We then store all of our calories as fat and become ravenous. More of the hormone ghrelin is released, which signals hunger, and we crave sugary foods and simple carbohydrates. In fact, the correlation between obesity and sleep deprivation can be seen when comparing maps of these two factors. So if you are looking to lose weight, be sure to get enough sleep so your appetite is better regulated, and you lose fat, not lean muscle.

DID YOU KNOW?

If a person is deprived of sleep for too long, they will die. Just a few years ago, scientists found that death is always preceded by the accumulation of molecules known as reactive oxidative species (ROS) in the gut. For obvious reasons, these studies could not be conducted on humans, but were done on fruit flies (which, would you believe, share many sleep-regulating genes with humans!) and confirmed the results with laboratory mice.[110]

Finally, getting a good night's sleep will even affect how appealing you are to others. One study showed that people prefer to avoid sleep-deprived folks, rating them less attractive and less healthy than when these same folks are well-rested.[111]

Maintaining healthy sleep habits is more than just nightly renewal. It's also recognizing that our active efforts need to be balanced with periods of complete rest, as the world's wisdom traditions have taught. In these quiet hours of relaxation, restoration, and recovery, we honor our bodies' needs and limitations, generating the energy required to greet the new day with vigor and enthusiasm. Without proper shut-eye, we limit our effectiveness and thwart the emotional and physical healing that comes with sleep. Proper rest enhances our capacities to connect with others, to be fully present and attentive to people we encounter. Sleep is not merely a biological need, but a profound practice that enables our lights to shine more brightly.

NATURE AND CREATION

The day I cease to be staggered by the star-salted blackness outside the window of a transatlantic flight—this portable mountaintop of body and mind—I shall have ceased to be human or alive.

—Maria Popova[112]

With each passing day and year, I find more and more solace in the company of trees. Most mornings and occasional evenings, I take a meditative walk through the woods near our home. When my mind is particularly active (another word for distracted!) during my morning sits, I take to the nearby trails and simply observe nature: the variety of barks on trees; the calls of the songbirds through the canopy; the towering evergreens toppled over and dying due to a fungal disease; the abundance of new evergreens springing up at the base of these older trees. I see every shade of green leaves, and I catch sight of deer off in the distance, their penetrating gaze following me. I walk and behold the wondrous natural world, noting the faint pine smell with more gratitude in my heart than I can fully express.

Day after day I walk, slowly inhaling each breath, filled with awe and thanksgiving. It is enough, this simple monastic ritual. "Look at the birds of the air," Jesus tells us in Matthew 6:26.[113] The poet Mary Oliver instructs us to "Pay attention. Be astonished. Tell about it." Writer Pico Iyer says, "In an age of acceleration, nothing can be more exhilarating than going slow. In an age of distraction, nothing is so luxurious as paying attention."

Medieval folklore tells a fanciful story about walking slowly in nature. When someone embarked on a leisurely stroll, they would say they were going to "Saint Terre," or the "Holy Land." This tale maintains that the earth became known, then, as "Saint Terre," and this is the origin for the word "saunter," to walk upon the earth with reverence. Even though this might not be a factual tale, it contains some truth!

> *Keep close to Nature's heart . . . and break clear away, once in a while, and climb a mountain or spend a week in the woods. Wash your spirit clean.*
>
> —John Muir

So I head to the "Holy Land" and saunter. And sometimes this is all I can do at the start of my day, as the world struggles with fires, disease, war, hunger, injustice, and suffering everywhere. I cannot afford to wallow in sadness or be overwhelmed. I walk. I look. I listen. And I tell myself it is okay to bask in this exquisite beauty for a few moments before tackling the day's challenges.

> *The moment one gives close attention to anything, even a blade of grass, it becomes a mysterious, awesome, indescribably magnificent world in itself.*
>
> —Henry Miller

These daily constitutions settle my mind and often provide flashes of insight or inspiration. One thing I know for sure: When I miss a day, my body and mind are not the same. I feel less grounded, less attentive, less creative, less able to handle the ups and downs of the day with equanimity. With all those benefits accruing from this simple activity, I hope to be able to continue as long as I live.

PRACTICE

Find a little spot of nature near you, a piece of "saint terre," where you can slow down, pay attention, and really look and listen.

Natural environments provide us with a host of benefits, from reducing stress hormones such as cortisol, to activating our "rest and digest" mode. After spending time in nature, we ruminate less, our moods improve, and depression and anxiety will likely fade. Even viewing trees and plants from a window has been linked to cognitive benefits. Japanese research shows that forest bathing (known as *shinrin-yoku*) boosts our immunity due to compounds called phytoncides that many varieties of trees release into the air.[114] Walking in nature improves our attention and memory skills, helping to restore cognitive functions.[115]

> *Nature does not ask for explanations, only that we witness the fleeting moment that is constant. Go for a walk in nature and receive the blessings of a tree, listen carefully for the cry of a bird, take counsel with a constant and abiding stream. Allow yourself to reconnect to the creative matrix that supports all of life.*
>
> —Robert A. Johnson and Jerry Ruhl

One overlooked benefit to spending time in nature is that our sense of time, which is inherently subjective, expands. A common malady of our modern world is the sense of time scarcity. We have too much to do and not enough time to do it, leading to higher stress levels.[116] But being in nature provides us a sense of "time richness," making us feel like we are gaining time. Whenever we focus on being attentive, this impacts our sense of time. When we are in natural landscapes, we may experience awe, which brings us into the present moment and adjusts our time perception. Researchers find that when we view spacious scenes, we feel time passing more slowly than when viewing cluttered ones.[117]

> *A bird does not sing because it has an answer, it sings because it has a song.*
>
> —Maya Angelou

Each spring day, the sun rises a bit earlier and the little warblers outside our bedroom window wake me up at exactly 5:20 a.m. Every. Single. Morning. Who needs a rooster when you have this gang of singers, reveling in their serenades and cacophony of sounds? If only I was a morning person who gladly jumped out of bed at that hour. But alas, I am not. So I resort to using earplugs to get additional much-needed beauty sleep. Then, at a more reasonable hour, I take my morning walk and listen to other chirpers.

Perhaps you have songbirds in your neighborhood, too. If not, I hope you can venture out to listen to a few. Why? Because birdsong does wonders for our psychological well-being. Researchers from King's College in London reported that hearing avian cheeps and chirps enhances our moods, relieves depression, and provides other mental health benefits for up to eight hours after hearing them.[118] Amazing, right? Another study from Berlin suggests that listening to birdsong improves anxiety, while hearing traffic noise is related to higher depressiveness.[119]

PRACTICE

A great way to tune into birdsong is by using the Merlin app on your phone, which will help you identify the birdsongs you are hearing and deepen your knowledge of the warblers in your area.

> *In order to see birds it is necessary to become a part of the silence.*
>
> —Robert Lynd

Birds can not only boost our mental health, but if we closely observe them, we can also discover some important lessons about confidence, parenting, group participation, attitude, and respect for natural resources as well as individuality.[120]

1. **Be confident:** Many bird parents build their nests and lay eggs on precarious ledges to avoid predators. The little chicks need to be quite daring to jump into the abyss as they learn to fly. Sometimes we need to be brave and leap out of our comfort zone to partake of a new experience or opportunity.

2. **Be a good parent:** Many birds will adopt some crazy antics to protect their young. For example, killdeer birds will pretend they are injured and flop around on the ground to attract a predator's attention away from their young. Corvids, such as crows and ravens, have greater success in raising their brood due to the time and devotion they spend on their fledglings. Parenting advice one would give to humans, as well.

3. **Nurture bonds with family and friends:** Many of us have witnessed the amazing aerial dances, or murmurations, of starlings. Thousands of birds turning, swirling, diving, and

swooping overhead in perfect formation. How and why do they accomplish this? Scientists believe this spectacle helps protect the birds from predators, while others say it strengthens existing bonds and helps to forge new ones. Studies have found that each bird reacts to the movements of six or seven neighbors, which maximizes the interplay between the group's cohesion and individual effort.[121]

4. **Be cheerful:** We can hear birds chirping outside our windows even on the dreariest of winter days in Pennsylvania. These warblers seem to be reminding us that no matter the weather, we can find something to be cheerful about.

5. **Recycle and reuse:** We've observed robins using and reusing a nest on our deck rafters for many years. They may bring in a few new sticks, but mostly they don't start from scratch.

6. **Celebrate differences:** Some birds like to work in teams, others by themselves. It's good to acknowledge that each of us is unique, and my way isn't necessarily better than yours—it may just be different.

> *To love creation means to perceive its beauty in the most unexpected places.*
>
> —Dorothee Sölle

When we go outside, researchers remind us to pay attention: It is easy to forget that birds are also there singing their hearts out. Nature reduces our body's stress levels while heightening our ability to focus. Birdwatchers who paid attention to the joy they felt for each bird reported greater mental health benefits than people who merely counted the birds they saw.

Try This

Carve out a few minutes today to listen to the birds wherever you find them. Your body, mind, and spirit will thank you!

My nose was to the grindstone during a particularly busy week in early September. I began my morning walk through the woods with my gaze fixed on the muddy path. I heard birdsong above and looked up into the tall trees. Ahhh, the tall trees and sky above! I realized I hadn't looked up much lately, both literally or figuratively. I then remembered Brother David Steindl-Rast's advice: "Look at the sky. We so rarely look at the sky, with clouds coming and going." I continued to look up as I walked along, and ten minutes later, almost on cue, a ten-foot branch careened onto the path ahead. I almost laughed. Okay! I got the message loud and clear! *Look up. Look up. Look up.*

Too often, I keep my head down and plow through the tasks at hand, failing to pause and notice the sky and trees. Autumn was approaching, the season that writer Pico Iyer says, "makes the least of us philosophical," teaching us that life is impermanent. So we had better take some moments to look at and see—really see—the clouds and the trees and leaves! I rededicated myself to that practice, and hope to continue avoiding falling trees on my path!

Try This

Today, may you take a moment to breathe and look up at the sky.

"What's the AQI this morning?" I now ask during some summer months before rolling out of bed. It's a measurement I barely knew existed a few years earlier. In our corner of the world, one summer, the air quality index was the most essential piece of information needed for the day.

Like many in the United States, those of us living in Pennsylvania have experienced unhealthy air quality due to forest fires. I'm someone who feels the effects of high AQIs in multiple ways, including congestion, tight chest, headache, and coughing. I'm homebound on those days and don't dare venture out, even if I were to wear two masks.

The most difficult part for me is the loss of my morning ritual of strolling through the woods. I miss all the benefits of morning sunlight, along with the calm and joy I experience listening to birds and gazing at the trees and sky.

The other lesson from our new AQI reality is the reminder once again of how connected we are to one another. The smoke we sometimes see in our skies usually originates from wildfires in Canada, far away from our home. It's a stark reminder of the work we must continue to do to save our earth from overheating. So as I grind my coffee beans each summer morning and name three things I am grateful for, a low AQI now takes a spot on the list.

Nature has always provided me with wonder and connection, allowing my busy mind to settle and my body to relax. It's not a surprise, then, that science has uncovered biological reasons why this is true for me and for billions of others. By humbly attending to all aspects of nature with childlike awe, we open ourselves up to its amazing sights, sounds, scents, and textures, healing our bodies, lifting our spirits, and relaxing our minds. Every intricate piece of our extraordinary, created world offers us the opportunity to contemplate our purpose and reconnect to our place in the web of life.

PART III

BRAINS

DISTRACTION, FOCUS, AND ATTENTION

You will never reach your destination if you stop and throw stones at every dog that barks.

—Winston Churchill

Our brains are of utmost importance for overall health and well-being. Despite comprising just 2 to 3 percent of our body weight, the brain requires 20 percent of both our oxygen and glucose intake. These fuel demands clearly indicate the crucial part our brains play in our survival. But people are not only concerned about their brains surviving, but truly thriving. Over and over again, audience members ask me: "How can I maintain my cognitive abilities as I grow older?"

In this chapter, we'll explore some of the most recent findings in neuroscience and brain health. This information will illustrate how incredibly amazing that three-pound globe atop your body really is. Here we go!

January is the month when I examine a few habits and practices to see where I need some improvement. One year, I decided to focus on my attention skills. Attention, and the lack of it, garners a lot of scrutiny in the media, so I added a few exercises to enhance awareness. I was feeling pretty good about my progress until a few weeks later, when I had a head-on collision with a ceiling fan. I had climbed atop a barstool to place a candle on a high shelf, carefully maintaining my balance as I crouched down, probably congratulating myself on my balancing act. I rose to stand on the chair and my head met the spinning blades of the nearby ceiling fan, sending two of them flying and crashing to the ground. Unfortunately, I had failed to notice the fan rotating at its highest speed. I was so focused on the candle placement that I never even saw it. I was stunned, not only from the impact, but also how hard my head must have been to sustain only a small cut and bump to show for all the drama. Obviously, I need a lot more practice in the attention skills area!

> *In an age of distraction, nothing can feel more luxurious than paying attention.*
>
> —Pico Iyer

Studies show that our minds are distracted about 50 percent of the time.[122] That means we are sleepwalking through half of our lives, our thoughts bouncing here and there, instead of focusing on the tasks at hand. (See my story for proof!) Our modern world bombards us with enticing diversions and information, leaving many of us exhausted by the overload; it also leaves us with the inability to focus for any length of time. Johann Hari helpfully classifies the four levels of attention as described below.[123]

1. **Flow:** deep immersion in a task and time flies by.

2. **Hyper-focus:** intense concentration on a task while blocking out distractions.

3. **Scattered focus:** easily distracted and frequent switching between tasks.

4. **Crisis mode:** stressed, difficult to focus, overwhelmed and constantly distracted.

Hari's recommendations on how to reclaim attention skills include many of the topics we're discussing here: getting adequate sleep, exercising regularly, spending time in nature, and practicing mindfulness. He also recommends reducing consumption of processed foods, eating a balanced diet, taking regular breaks, and setting boundaries with social media and digital devices.

> *Tell me what you pay attention to and I will tell you who you are.*
>
> —José Ortega y Gasset

Selective attention is important. The act of ignoring is far more important than most realize, and it is a very active process. It takes cognitive resources to filter out irrelevant information. We want to focus, but we also need to ignore inputs. But focusing and ignoring are two different processes. Just because we are focusing on something does not mean we are successfully ignoring another thing.

Older adults do as well as twenty-year-olds for taking in relevant information. But they suffer deficits when trying to ignore irrelevant details; older adults are simply more distractible than younger adults. This is why our son can work on a complex philosophy paper in a noisy coffeehouse, and I struggle to write a coherent sentence. This difficulty is caused by structural changes in the middle of the prefrontal cortex, the part of your brain just behind your forehead. This area plays a crucial role in attention control, and is the site of other executive functions like planning and organizing, decision-making, impulse control, and emotional regulation.

As we age, white matter in the prefrontal cortex degrades, so ignoring irrelevant information becomes slower.[124] The good news is that we can hold some of this degradation at bay by practicing meditation or silent prayer. The white matter of long-term pray-ers and meditators tends to be better preserved. Just another reason to commit ourselves to one of these practices, for the benefit of both our brains and our spirits.

> *Bringing back a wandering attention, over and over again, is the very root of judgment, character, and will.*
>
> —William James

DID YOU KNOW?

As we grow older, it often becomes harder to retain the information we learn. Here are four ways to reduce distractions and improve focusing skills.[125]

1. During conversations, look at the person who is speaking and be attentive to what they are saying. Ask them to repeat anything you may have missed.

2. Rephrase and reiterate. Put what you are hearing into your own words, to embed the information into your memory.

3. Remember that as we age, our ability to disregard distractions becomes more difficult. Be cognizant of the noise level in your environment, and seek quiet areas to hold conversations.

4. Doing one task at a time and avoiding interruptions will enhance your ability to focus.

> *Stop measuring days by degree of productivity and start experiencing them by degree of presence.*
>
> —Alan Watts

Multitasking has been shown to be unhelpful for a number of reasons. When we are multitasking we are actually task-switching, or moving our attention back and forth between two or more activities. Studies suggest we lose up to 40 percent of our productive time when we frequently change tasks.[126] Work quality is lower, errors are more frequent, and mental strain is higher. We may feel efficient, but that feeling is misleading. However, if one of the activities is mindless, like folding laundry or taking bites of a sandwich, we can effectively do two things at once. But researchers find that when people multitask while doing a pleasant activity like eating, they enjoy the meal less and experience what they call a hedonic shortfall. This leads to a pleasure deficit, prompting overconsumption of food, alcohol, social media scrolling, or gaming activities later on. Instead, if we can focus on how the sandwich tastes, for example, we fully enjoy the meal and find no need to fill up on other pleasurable activities later.

Try This

Are you guilty of attempting to complete two or more tasks at once? Do you get distracted by pings and rings frequently? If so, turn off notifications when you are working on important tasks. Or put away your phone or laptop when eating a meal and turn your attention to your taste buds. It takes some discipline, but I've found the work flows better and I enjoy meals much more!

Would you believe that indoor temperatures can affect attentional ability in your later years? A groundbreaking study showed that indoor temperatures and cognitive performance are closely related. Holding the dial between 68–75 °F (20–24 °C) on the thermostat helps stave off attention declines in older adults. What an easy way to support our brain health![127]

> *Be happy for this moment. This moment is your life.*
>
> —Omar Khayyam

One of the ways I have been attentive all through my life is by collecting rocks wherever I go. I began this practice as a young girl during family vacations. We occasionally traveled with my dad's best friend and his family: nine kids and four adults in all. What great memories I have of those trips! Uncle Burt, a geology teacher, instilled in me a curiosity about rocks, their formation, and their history. Because of his influence, I'm always on the lookout for unique stones when I tread newfound paths. I tuck them away in my pockets and bring them home (when, of course, it's permissible), where they find a place among all of my collected stones. They serve as reminders to be grateful and observe even the smallest wonders of nature.

The shoreline of Lake Michigan has the most beautiful collection of smooth-edged stones, and I've been fortunate to visit the sandy beach below the Racine Retreat Center in Wisconsin. Although I already have more than enough stones, I cannot resist picking up a few more when I am there. They remind me of the slow pace of nature. Lake Michigan was formed after the last ice age, around 14,000 years ago, and these rocks have been gradually buffed smooth as they tumble against one another in the waves. This process takes years, even decades, depending on their sizes. These stones remind me that I need to be patient with myself and all the changes I hope to make in my life. It takes a long time to wear away jagged edges, literally and figuratively. We don't have 14,000 years to work with, so relax and do your best.

> *Some people get addicted to chain-smoking their problems. They spend all day going from sorrow to sorrow. It doesn't have to be that way. You can live each day going from joy to joy—like a sunflower that turns to face the sun as it moves across the sky. It's not about having a problem-free life, but about focusing on the light. Sunflowers still have shadows, but they are always behind them.*
>
> —James Clear[128]

The Dutch have a practice called *niksen*, the practice of "purposefully doing nothing" that can decrease anxiety and boost creativity and productivity.[129] Scans show that more brain areas communicate with each other when we are letting our minds wander for a bit.[130] How to do it?

Try This

Sit or stand by a window and look out on nature, up at the sky, or people passing by.

What do you see? Just spend several minutes simply looking at the objects without analyzing them. If your mind wanders away, notice that and bring your attention back to just sitting there with nothing to do. Without judging or mentally engaging, listen to the birds or wind in the trees. Just "be." You'll find your stress decreases, chatter lessens, and your happiness increases.

> *If you believe that feeling bad or worrying long enough will change a past or future event, then you are residing on another planet with a different reality system.*
>
> —William James

It's no wonder the people of Holland are some of the most satisfied on earth. We also might remember that several biblical passages contain the phrase, "Be still." It's a simple, profound lesson that has been carried out through millennia.

> *The way in which we go to the grocery store may tell us everything about the way in which we live a life.*
>
> —Rachel Naomi Remen

James Williams, a Google executive for many years, became horrified by what their products were doing to our attention. He left Google and became an ambassador for attentional maintenance.[131] He says there are three layers of attention: The first is daylight. For example, you narrow your focus to complete a task, like baking cookies. You enter your kitchen, find the ingredients in your cupboard, turn on the oven, mix the batter, put the cookie dough balls into the oven, take them out, and try not to eat every last one. Daylight is what we are focusing on right now, at this moment.

The second layer is what he calls "starlight," which is your focus on long-term goals and values: Be an honest human being, a good parent, save money for retirement, train for a marathon, etc. When you lose sight of that goal, you look up, figuratively, at the stars and realign your actions towards those goals. It continually asks, "Who do I want to be, and what do I want to accomplish?" If you lose your sense of starlight, you no longer know what you want to do in your life. I sometimes ask myself simple questions: "Are my actions reflecting a woman of integrity? Am I being compassionate and understanding?" I want to live as an honorable person and align my actions with these long-term goals.

His third layer is what he names "spotlight," our short-term attention that gets hijacked by dings and pings and rings arriving all day long. It is reactive and not reflective and can shift continually as we go about our day. Instead of focusing on long-term projects and goals, our spotlight jumps from one shiny thing to another. And Williams says that our devices are wired to keep this spotlight attention bopping around, often below our conscious control.

> *In every struggle there is a hidden blessing.*
>
> —Joan Chittister, O.S.B.

Distraction happens to all of us. And when it happens to me, I find it's an opportunity to practice self-acceptance and perhaps find hidden blessings somewhere. One afternoon, I was readying a few extra bins filled with card orders to take to our post office before the 5:00 p.m. pickup. I knelt next to the three bins to consolidate them into two, and as I picked up one large envelope (destination Canada), the tape came off the corner. So I got up and brought the package to the card-folding room to re-tape it. As I was doing so, the phone rang in the other room. I jumped up, answered the phone, talked to the customer for a few minutes, then resumed organizing the bins. I carried the bins to the car and drove to the post office with almost thirty minutes to spare. I was feeling good.

When I returned to the office, however, I saw the international envelope sitting on the table. I'd forgotten to finish the re-taping after being interrupted by the phone call. And now I would need to head back to the post office to catch the last pickup. Ugh.

I was upset that I got distracted by the phone call and failed to take this package with me on the first trip. But I paused for a few seconds and remembered my own advice: Take a deep breath and just do what needs to be done. Give yourself a break. It's no big deal. Drive the car and be grateful you have a car to drive and that you discovered the mistake in time. This is no big deal. (I said that to myself more than a few times!) I made sure to look upward and admire the sky, which was displaying some brilliant shades of gold, pink, and violet as the sun began to set. After dropping off the package, I took a short walk through the woods nearby, and had a delightful conversation with another woman, sharing our awe and amazement at the radiant sunset. The day ended on a beautiful note.

This experience reminded me—again—to take life as it comes. Getting upset at my mistakes and shortcomings does not help in any way but only serves to cause unnecessary suffering. Remember that none of us is perfect; we are all human. And the sooner we let go of blaming ourselves, the better off our minds and bodies will be.

> *Attention is the most basic form of love.*
>
> —John Tarrant

Attentiveness is a skill and a gift, and practicing it will bring many rewards. Neuroscientist Amishi Jha, PhD, notes that when we attend to the person in front of us and offer our sincere interest, we are saying, "I see you. I care about you. You are important to me."[132] That simple acknowledgement is a gift in our automated, anonymous world.

Similarly, when we anchor our attention on everyday blessings, we actually hear the birds chirp, we see our friends smile, we note the subtle sweetness in our cup of tea. Yes, there are distractions and struggles and heartaches and difficulties in all our lives. But there are also gifts to behold, and it only takes a moment to pause throughout the day, to listen and carefully observe them. We can take author Tim Roberts's advice to "see beyond what's broken to the beauty and wholeness of life." Amen to that!

Try This

Take a moment to attend to beauty and wholeness right now. What do you see right in front of you and around you? No matter how ordinary the objects may be, their colors and shapes might hold unique bits of beauty. Notice that before continuing with your day.

CHATTER

If your distress has some external cause, it is not the thing itself that troubles you, but your own judgment of it—and you can erase this immediately.

—Marcus Aurelius

I've noticed that one of my worst habits, and one of the few I will admit to, is waking up and, before even getting out of bed, thinking of the thousand and one tasks I hope to tackle. What a terrible way to start the day! I should know better! I often catch myself, but sometimes I don't quiet my internal chatter until I'm taking my morning meditative walk.

DID YOU KNOW?

Did you know that on average, we talk to ourselves at a rate of about 4,000 words per minute? Think about that for a moment. That voice in our heads is a really, really fast talker!

A few years ago, we moved our home and business in just two weeks, and that inner voice worked overtime with a to-do list a mile long. It seemed overwhelming, to put it mildly. But then I would notice and step back, realizing that the stress I felt was simply due to my thoughts. And those anxious thoughts weren't contributing to the packing effort! In fact, they were probably slowing the process. My niece Alison likens chatter to her computer running a program in the background, taking up energy and bandwidth, but not offering anything positive to her work efforts.

Neuroscientist and psychologist Ethan Kross discusses our internal dialogues and the harm and stress they can cause.[133] He emphasizes that the way we talk to ourselves is vitally important. We might worry about future events, ruminate over past experiences, or cycle through negative thoughts and anxieties. If distressing thoughts are continuous, our bodies handle this psychological stress like we handle physical stressors. Inflammation rises, and we are more susceptible to illness and infections. Professor Steve Cole of UCLA calls this chatter effect "death at the molecular level."

Kross recommends using "you" instead of "I" when talking to ourselves, which creates psychological distance. So I would say to myself, "You are feeling stressed, Anne," anchoring me in "observer" mode. By taking a step back mentally, we are better able to view our problems objectively, helping reduce anxiety. It also allows us to frame the issues at hand as challenges instead of threats. That reframing produces a much healthier outcome for our hearts and blood pressures, too. In both challenging and threatening situations, our hearts beat faster. But our blood vessels react very differently. When we imagine we are under threat, our blood vessels constrict, which can lead to serious problems in our cardiovascular system over time. But if we shift to a challenge mindset, our blood vessels relax, which is a much better scenario for our physical and emotional well-being.

We can also tamp down the ill effects of chatter by going into nature, exercising, talking with a friend, or immersing oneself in a ritual like cleaning or organizing a room. Kross has found, though, that simply ruminating with another person is unlikely to provide relief. It's best to have someone help us reframe the issues we are facing, since simply poring over the situation does not ease anxiety or discomfort.

Increasing my awareness of that busy inner voice has been very helpful to me, particularly during stressful times. I talk to "Anne" like I would an old friend, encouraging her to send those worrisome thoughts down the river, releasing the background noise. This practice soothes my unease, nudging me toward more productive efforts. I invite you to try it for yourself and see the difference it makes!

TRY THIS

As you go about your week, stop a few times each day to notice your thoughts. Have you been swept up in a merry-go-round of chatter? Are you ruminating on a past conversation or unresolved difficulty? Stopping to notice our thoughts is the first step towards releasing them and bringing our attention back to the present moment, where joy can be experienced.

> *Remember: A wandering mind is an unhappy mind.*
>
> —MATT KILLINGSWORTH

> *Each moment we are fully paying attention is an atom of eternity. The quality of our attention measures the quantity of our aliveness.*
>
> —MARIA POPOVA

THE MATURING BRAIN

Aging is not the passive, inevitable march of decay we once thought it was. Our neural architecture continues to rewrite itself until our final days, responding to how we challenge it, nourish it, and engage with the world around us.

—Elkhonon Goldberg

For most adults, learning and thinking skills plateau between thirty and forty years old, and then begin to diminish. Cognitive skills like processing speed decline, and after the age of sixty, this slide becomes steeper. But scientists have found a way to reverse that decline. A three-month study found that by providing participants with an enriched learning environment (learning computer skills, music, photography, foreign language, etc.) for six hours per week, the subjects improved their memory and attention so much that their abilities began to match with people thirty years younger.[134] The participants took three two-hour classes per week and improved their cognitive skills for memory and attention. Remarkably, one year later, the improvement had increased by another twenty years: Their brains were now functioning like they were fifty years younger! The researchers postulated that the "normal" cognitive slide found in older adults can be attributed to the same kind of decline that occurs in children during summer breaks: Their abilities diminish only because they aren't acquiring new skills like they do during the school year.

The term "superagers" is often used to identify older individuals who circumvent the normal cognitive decline associated with aging. They are able to maintain stable cognitive performance in both memory and non-memory areas well into their eighties and nineties. A recent study examined their brains to see how they differed from age-matched control groups. Scientists discovered that structures in the white matter of superagers' brains did not show the same decline as others in their age group. These superagers had better physical and mental health, and a higher interest in music.[135] Neuroscientists note four essential habits that will sustain our cognitive health as we age:

1. **Good sleep hygiene:** Keep a consistent schedule and sleep seven to eight hours per night. (More info can be found in the "Bodies" section in the Sleep chapter.)

2. **Regular physical exercise:** Scientists found that subjects' verbal fluency improved after just an hour per week of vigorous exercise.[136] The increased blood flow to the brain is most likely responsible for this boost in cognition.

3. **Social interactions:** So many studies conclude that this is the most important habit![137]

4. **Mental challenges:** Some examples include music, reading, puzzles, and hobbies. My favorite daily puzzle challenge is the "Connections" game from the *New York Times.*

The message is clear: We have more control over how our brains age than we ever thought. So keep active, both physically and mentally, and you will reap the benefits. Maintaining your brain's cognitive functions isn't complicated. Just continue moving and learning.[138]

DID YOU KNOW?

Research shows the following five practices can stave off dementia.[139] You will notice these recommendations duplicate advice for nurturing a variety of brain and body functions.

1. **Exercise:** Even walking just a few minutes every day can provide many benefits: better stamina, strength, stress management, and immune function. But the main reason movement helps our brains is that it reduces inflammation and promotes the function and growth of neural cells. Inactivity is probably the most significant risk factor in dementia. Try turning your walk into a meditation or prayer pause for even more benefits.

2. **Sleep:** Getting seven to eight hours each night seems to clear the brain of debris that might otherwise build up and create problems.

3. **Have a sense of purpose:** People who have meaningful activities and goals to accomplish reduce their risk of suffering the deleterious effects of dementia.

4. **Eat well:** Mediterranean diets are recommended, which are rich in vegetables, berries, beans, whole grains, fish, poultry, and olive oil.

5. **Stay social:** Nurture close relationships, which may help you live longer and are important for brain health. Volunteering and serving others is shown to be particularly helpful in maintaining health throughout the lifespan. Loneliness seems to be a factor in developing Alzheimer's.

As someone who enjoys aerobic exercise, I was happy to hear that a 2019 study found that short bouts of aerobic exercise can improve working memory as much as caffeine.[140] Both caffeine and exercise are known to improve certain aspects of cognition, like attention and alertness. Brisk walks—even as short as twenty minutes—can provide your working memory with just as much pep as that morning cup of coffee. (But I enjoy both!) Exercise can also help curb the negative effects of caffeine withdrawal, such as fatigue, headaches, and bad moods.[141]

TRY THIS

Explore just one of the recommended practices this week. Start small. For example, take a walk for just two to five minutes each morning. Or add one meatless meal to your weekly menu, emphasizing protein and vegetables. Or go to bed earlier, aiming for seven to eight hours of shut-eye. See if you don't feel better after just one week of the practice.

We've explored many ways to incorporate brain-healthy habits into our everyday lives. Don't try to tackle them all at once. Some habits will feel more natural to adopt than others, so just do your best and practice self-compassion. In time, your brain and body will thank you!

DEPRESSION AND ANXIETY

One discovers the light in darkness. . . . It is necessary, while in darkness, to know that there is a light somewhere, to know that in oneself, waiting to be found, there is a light.

—James Baldwin

According to the Journal of the American Medical Association (JAMA), approximately 9 percent of American adults experience major depression each year, with a lifetime prevalence of approximately 20 percent for men and 33 percent for women.[142] In any given year, approximately 21–40 million American adults suffer from depression or anxiety.[143] These are sobering statistics, reminding us that millions of people struggle with mental health issues. Most of us have been touched by this common ailment, either ourselves or through family and friends. I have children, nieces, siblings, cousins, and friends who have suffered with depression and anxiety, so have seen firsthand how difficult it is to climb out of this abyss of misery.

DID YOU KNOW?

Unfortunately, mental health issues impact our brains in numerous ways:

1. The hippocampus, an important brain area for memory and emotional regulation, can shrink in volume.

2. The prefrontal cortex, site of several executive functions, including planning and complex thinking, can contract and become less active.

3. The amygdala can become overactive, causing exaggerated responses to fear and negative stimuli.

4. Imbalances in neurotransmitters can negatively affect mood, attention, and stress regulation.

5. Increased inflammation in the brain can lead to cell damage and cognitive impairment.

Consulting mental health professionals is always recommended, but we also know that there are proven wellness practices that can help in managing depression. Many of these practices are addressed in other sections of this book. A brief list would include exercise, meditation, quality sleep, diet, and relationships, along with spending time outside in nature.

Not surprisingly, women experience higher levels of anxiety, depression, and sleep issues than men, despite gains in freedom and employment opportunities.[144] A key factor contributing to these issues, besides brain structure differences and hormonal fluctuations, may be their dissatisfaction with how society views and treats women.[145] I was an engineering student and varsity volleyball player in the late seventies and early eighties, engulfed in an atmosphere of overt sexism and discrimination. For instance, the engineering school building at the University of Missouri did not have a women's bathroom on the first floor when I arrived as a freshman student in 1976. In the next year, someone thought a good remedy would be to simply slap a new sign on one of the men's rooms. Thus our "new" women's bathroom had urinals and one stall. A few professors even asked what I planned to do with my engineering degree upon graduation. Really? Did they ask any of my male classmates that question? And although the male athletes received academic assistance and accommodations along with adaptable mealtimes, I was penalized for missed classes and labs due to games, tournaments, and travel. When women athletes missed hot meals, we packed cold cut sandwiches.

Luckily, the sexism I endured in those years did not produce depressive symptoms in me. But my exercise habits certainly helped maintain my positive mental state; I ran long distances after volleyball season, completing two marathons while in college. Participating in both of those sports also aided my interoception development. What the heck is interoception? It's the ability to sense what is going on in one's body. You might think, "Of course I know what's going on inside my body. Doesn't everyone?" Not exactly. Interoception is a skill that varies widely among individuals. It allows us to sense if we are hungry or sated, hot or cold, tense or relaxed. The more important feature to appreciate is that interoception is crucial to supporting our moods. The more we move our bodies, the more interoceptive we become. We are better at regulating emotions, predicting physiological needs, and improving our overall body awareness.

Scientists have studied interoception as it relates to depression.[146] Remarkably, they have discovered that people who are skilled at this sensory awareness have better moods than people who are less skilled. People who are depressed or anxious often ruminate on troubling thoughts, creating an endless loop of negativity. But this cycle can be interrupted by focusing on a physical action such as counting one's inhalations and exhalations. Or you could notice the sun on your skin, the touch of your fingers on a keyboard, or the weight of your sit bones on a chair.

When leading my yoga classes, I often begin and end with cues related to breathing: "Inhale through your nose and lengthen your exhalations through your mouth. Think about each exhale releasing any tension or discomfort you may have." These instructions are meant to engender calm in the students' bodies and enhance awareness of their internal feelings. Students sometimes report that they had never noticed the stress they were carrying in their bodies, and these breathing exercises help them release tightness and boost their sense of peace.

TRY THIS

Sit up tall, with one hand on each thigh. Maintain a calm steady breathing pattern, and slowly tap each thigh, alternating right and left. Count the taps up to ten, then count back down to one.

This technique is helpful because it engages both sides of the brain and body, and it provides a physical focal point to help interrupt anxious thoughts and feelings.

By developing our bodily awareness, we can create an early warning system that helps prevent depression and anxiety from taking hold. Simply pausing several times during the day, noting what we are feeling, and taking a few deep breaths is one of the best ways to stay in tune with our bodies and minds. Cultivating this mind-body connection enables us to recognize emerging anxieties so that we respond with appropriate self-care before they escalate into deeper issues. This breath practice can reset our attention and invite calm into the moment.

STRUGGLE AND GRIT

Fall seven times, stand up eight.

—JAPANESE PROVERB

One of my greeting cards contains the following saying by Albert Einstein: "In the middle of difficulty lies opportunity." Although it isn't a best-seller, many customers find the message meaningful, because when we look back on our lives, we often find that the most difficult challenges we encountered provided new perspectives and introspection. Of course, while we are going through difficulties, gratitude for inner growth is not top of mind. But there are effective practices that are valuable in times of stress, grief, or other difficulties. When we put them into practice, we can develop the resilience to handle these challenges more easily, and bounce back more rapidly after upsetting events.

What are some mindfulness practices that can support us through these tough times? The first is to simply be more mindful of the present moment: Focus your attention on this very moment and ask yourself, "What is true in this moment?" Then pause and breathe for a minute. Relax your body as you breathe and rest in this moment, without judging yourself or your thoughts. Just accept what is. You might want to notice what thoughts arise, and see if you can let go of them. Living in the present is very helpful, particularly when challenges arise and the future is uncertain.

Then, look for opportunities to share kindness. Research suggests that people who volunteer regularly tend to be happier and live longer than people who don't.[147] Even a small act of kindness can boost our mood and bring happiness to another. In addition, when we send our attention outward, caring for others whose struggles are considerable, we often forget our troubles or discover they are not so heavy.

Remember, too, that self-care is an act of compassion. Notice when world events or everyday life gets overwhelming. Stop and bring attention to your thoughts. Take a breath or two. If more is needed, go for a walk, listen to music, call a friend, do the dishes—choose any activity that will recenter yourself, giving yourself the care you deserve. Sure, we may not like our situation, but we do need to accept it. Welcome it all. Openly welcoming the good and bad times as equally valid experiences brings a balance and gentle calm to our lives. Practice allowing both pleasant and unpleasant experiences to come and go without resistance or struggle.

And finally, be grateful. Practicing gratitude is an antidote to our negativity bias, and grounds us in the moment. Our brains are wired to pay attention to danger and difficulty, which was helpful to our ancestors and kept them alive. But we often overidentify with our problems, and gratitude can thwart that tendency. Find just one or two things to be grateful for, even in the midst of struggle. Remember Brother David Steindl-Rast's advice: "Be grateful *in* situations, not necessarily *for* situations."

Try This

"Just for now. . ." is a phrase we might want to say to ourselves often. For example, "Just for now, I will enjoy this cup of tea and not allow the worries of the day to upend this peacefulness." "Just for now, I will find one thing to be grateful for in the midst of this difficulty." "Just for now, I will remain in this moment of contentment."

Scientists are studying the anterior midcingulate cortex (aMCC), an area of the brain that is the control center for tenacity, perseverance, and resolve. The more we perform tasks that are difficult, distasteful, or exhausting, this important brain region will grow.[148] When we tackle an item on our to-do list that we would rather put off forever, our aMCC is strengthened, along with our willpower. Studies show that in athletes and high-achieving students and professionals, this area of the brain is larger than normal. In obese individuals, the area is smaller.

The lesson to be learned here is to take on challenges regularly. If life gets too easy and comfortable, our brains shrink in size. When difficulties arise, we are then less able to handle them. And, sorry to say, none of us can expect a perfectly smooth ride in life. Taking on and persevering in small chores is how to keep our minds primed to handle bigger challenges. It's like anything and everything else: Use it or lose it.

TRAUMA

That which does not kill us makes us stronger.

—Friedrich Nietzsche

Thousands of research studies have been published on the topic of trauma, which impacts the brains and bodies of people who have experienced it. Trauma comes in many forms: It may be a one-time event, a repetitive, continuous experience, or something in between. Some people suffer from post-traumatic stress disorder (PTSD) following trauma, but others bounce back with little to no lingering effects.

The brain is impacted in several ways after a traumatic experience. The amygdala becomes hypervigilant, on high alert for threats and danger. It behaves like a smoke alarm going off constantly, even though it only detects a puff of smoke in the air. The hippocampus, a memory center in the brain, may shrink after trauma, affecting both short- and long-term memory. The prefrontal cortex, responsible for decision-making and emotional regulation, becomes less active. Making rational choices and keeping emotions in check become more difficult.

The stress associated with trauma causes levels of cortisol to stay elevated, resulting in mental and physical exhaustion in survivors. Serious health issues may arise from the effects of this constant tension like sleep disturbances, learning and relationship challenges, and an assortment of physical and emotional difficulties. When people experience trauma, they also often feel isolated from others, believing that no one will understand their reactions to what happened to them. They may only be willing to share their feelings with people who have suffered a similar injury. For many years, counseling professionals believed that verbally processing trauma was vital for recovery. But recent research shows that survivors who choose not to talk about their trauma can recover just as successfully as people who do. Coping styles are simply quite individual.[149]

There is some good news from trauma survivors, though: All these deleterious effects are not permanent if the victim receives proper care. The brain is adaptable, thank goodness, and if treatment addresses both the psychological and physical symptoms, the person can be healed. Amazingly, many who have recovered from traumatic events go on to use their experience to connect with and help others who are suffering. Their hard-won self-knowledge and inner strength provide a springboard to transform a terrible ordeal into a gift for others.

MEDITATION

Meditation is the ultimate mobile device; you can use it anywhere, anytime, unobtrusively.

—Sharon Salzberg

Each of us experienced small and large adversities during the COVID-19 pandemic, some rising to the level of trauma. This worldwide crisis reminded us that we all need something to steady ourselves when faced with uncontrollable circumstances. My friend and college roommate, Jill, an emergency room doctor, suffered mightily during that time. As a triathlete, she continued swimming every day to help manage the chaos that swirled around her at the hospital. Swimming with a snorkel, Jill spent hours simply observing the sun sparkling in the water. That, she said, was her meditation time and practice, and helped her continue serving her patients with kindness and compassion.

Is it possible to look at each challenge we face with clear eyes and ask, "What can I learn from this? Is there a valuable lesson here that I need to contemplate, such as greater patience and understanding, or deeper compassion and empathy?" Without a practice like silence, music, art, prayer, meditation, or writing, it can be difficult for wisdom to emerge from chaos.

The older I grow, the more I cherish silence. One of my favorite ways to enjoy moments of quiet is to do a walking meditation.[150] I'm not very good at sitting for more than twenty minutes, so this form of meditation works perfectly for me. To practice this properly, we don't just put one foot in front of the other mindlessly. Meditative walking is a deliberate, thoughtful practice, one I often teach in my workshops. Many people find this form of meditation soothing and helpful, while a few find it difficult. What is quite appealing about this practice is that most of us walk every day, and we can turn any walk into a meditation: a walk up and down the steps in your home, a walk through a hallway at work, or perhaps a walk from your car to the office or store. Anytime you walk, your focus can be turned toward each step, or your breath, and voila! You are meditating while moving!

> *Each mindful step reminds us that we are alive on this beautiful planet.*
>
> —Thich Nhat Hanh

TRY THIS

You might want to give walking meditation a try and see if it works for you. Here are three different ways to get started:

1. When we begin a walk with awareness, we've already changed our mindset and focus. Bring your attention to your breath. Either count how many breaths you take with each step, or how many steps you take with each breath, depending on how fast you walk and breathe. Just notice your breath and each step you take and the fact that you are alive. Nhat Hanh suggests adding a phrase like, "Breathing in, I calm my body. Breathing out, I bring peace into my body." Coordinate this saying with each in and out breath. When you practice in this way, you are cultivating mindfulness.

2. Deliberately think about your feet, your weight shifting as you take each step, performing every action intentionally that you usually do automatically. You will most likely need to slow down your movements in this method. Here, we simply take note of every small change in each foot as we move forward.

3. Try to notice these components of each step:

   a. lifting the heel of the back foot, coming on to your toes;

   b. raising that foot and moving it forward as your weight begins to shift;

   c. lowering the foot to the floor, slightly ahead of you, heel first;

   d. shifting your body weight onto your forward foot and leg.

   e. Lift your back heel and continue this deliberate movement.

During your walk, tune in to any sensations you might normally overlook: your breath coming in and out of your nose and mouth, your feet and legs moving forward, or the contact of your feet with the floor. Observe your head poised atop your neck and shoulders. Notice the nearby sounds and those created by the movement of your body. Take in whatever you see about you. When your mind wanders, as minds often do, relax and congratulate yourself for noticing. This is completely normal. Do not become upset. Gently guide it back to one of these sensations. Begin again by focusing on your weight shifting from one foot to another as you continue taking slow, mindful steps.

Walking meditation is an example of how we can use physical cues and sensations to enhance our prayer and our mindfulness. When I was a young girl, our Catholic school teachers provided suggestions for Lenten abstinence, hoping that this practice would help us keep our minds more focused on God. Their recommendations mostly centered on physical treats, like giving up candy, cake, gum, or ice cream. Every time we thought about that treat, we were to say a prayer, and perhaps drop some pennies into our "pagan baby" box. (That's a story for another time!) I usually gave up candy or cookies, but I can't confidently report that I prayed every time I reached for the cookie jar. Late into my teens I discovered that some believed there was an exception for the practice: Lent did not necessarily include Sundays, so one could "cheat" every seven days. That just seemed too easy for my sensibilities, so I kept to the program even on those days. (I don't need to tell you that I'm a recovering perfectionist.) But the lesson I learned was that physical cues and challenges are excellent aids in nurturing our spiritual lives.

Today, I still think of Lent as a season of opportunity for spiritual growth. It is celebrated during springtime in the northern hemisphere, with new life springing up all around us, which means there's a visible, natural connection to the Lenten season of cultivating new practices and habits. Aristotle said, "We are what we repeatedly do." Perhaps, like me, you have a habit you'd like to change, or one you'd like to begin. But during spring and the season of Lent, I've veered away from "giving up" and moved toward *metanoia*, the Greek word meaning "change of heart and mind." One need not be a religious person to find value in this practice. We can ask ourselves questions like: In what ways can we live with greater love and awareness? Put on the mind of a monk? Act with heartfelt compassion and care? Those questions are definitely more challenging than counting the days until I can eat chocolate chip cookies again!

These days, I might dedicate the days of Lent to nurturing my meditation practice, perhaps adding extra minutes to my daily walk or heading out a second time at sunset. I might challenge myself to resist being judgmental or show greater generosity and patience with people around me. I ask myself, "In what ways do I need to 'change my heart and mind?'"

Author James Clear reminds us: "In times of uncertainty, your habits can ground you. When you feel overwhelmed, practice one minute of mindfulness. When you feel restless, do a one-minute workout. When the world seems uncontrollable, focus on what you can control. Which of my current habits serves me most? Which serves me least?"[151]

It's important to keep in mind to start small, with just one habit, and work on that for a few weeks or longer. When the new habit becomes second nature, move on to another one. If we try to change too much all at once, we set ourselves up for failure. I need to remind myself of that, too!

TRY THIS

Contemplate one way you would like to cultivate a change of heart. Is there a quality or habit you'd like to foster, or a practice you'd like to develop? Think about that characteristic and take one small step to nurture it.

> *Ultimately, we have just one moral duty: to reclaim large areas of peace in ourselves, more and more peace, and to reflect it toward others. And the more peace there is in us, the more peace there will also be in our troubled world.*
>
> —Etty Hillesum[152]

One winter morning, I woke up thinking about habits I'd like to develop. I decided that nurturing more peace in my days would be helpful, and so I'd take on the mind of a monk, or at least what I imagined it might be. I would tend to my duties as if living in a monastery, performing every action with slow intention. (My monk friends laughed when I shared these thoughts with them.) I would not rush or take any side trips with meandering chatter. I would simply "be" with the washing and writing, the paperwork and planning, and be grateful, finding the joy in the utter simplicity of the present moment. This practice was not as easy as it sounds. By afternoon, I'd forgotten my intention, caught up in my thoughts and duties, so I regrouped and returned to placing my focus solely on each activity.

The idea for this exercise occurred to me after a conversation with a woman battling cancer. She is uncertain how much time she has; it may be only months, but she's hoping for two more years. I held that thought in mind for a few days. What would it be like to live each day, knowing it might be one of my last? Would I waste it by robotically checking items off a to-do list? Of course not. I would cherish every minute I had, taking in the ordinary with new eyes. But do I need a terminal diagnosis to live like this, having deep gratitude for every single moment?

Although volumes have been written about mindfulness, one mindful practice that was introduced to me just a few years ago is the notion of "savoring." Savoring is an effective mindfulness activity to enhance and prolong positive experiences and ground ourselves in the present.[153] I practice this in the morning while brewing a cup of coffee: I open the bag, breathe in the rich bouquet of roasted beans, drop the beans into the grinder, listen to the whir, pour hot water over the ground coffee, watch steam rise over the mug, warm the milk and slowly blend it into the coffee. I close my eyes, feel the warmth of the cup, and deeply breathe the nutty, robust aroma. Finally, I sip the toasty beverage with a grateful heart.

As we move through our days, many small moments become opportunities to practice. We can savor the sweet scent of lavender hand soap; admire the fluttering leaves on the trees; notice the soft feel of the chair cushion. Bit by bit, we build attentiveness and mindfulness into the day. The more frequently we practice these simple pauses, the more we nourish our brains, bodies, and spirits.

TRY THIS

- Choose an experience you want to savor.
- Slow your breath and thoughts.
- Focus on the positive aspects of the event, utilizing each of your senses.
- Stay present and reflect on how and why this experience is meaningful.
- Share your thoughts with others, and why they are pleasant for you.
- Focus on details you want to remember, creating a vivid memory.
- Express gratitude, verbally or in writing, for the event.
- Avoid overthinking and analyzing the experience.
- Practice savoring every day, even with small pleasures.

One of the proven practices for nurturing presence, attentiveness, and peace is coloring. Recent research has confirmed that coloring can be considered a mindfulness activity. It focuses our attention, keeping us rooted in the present moment while distracting us from any worries we may be carrying around about the past and the future. "Although the activity might be simple, our research has shown coloring really can be an effective way of reducing stress and improving well-being. We've shown that coloring is an easy way to lower anxiety and reduce burnout," write psychologists Michail Mantzios and Kyriaki Giannou.[154] If you are interested in coloring mindfully, here are a few tips to set you up for success.

TRY THIS

1. ***Find a quiet space and set an intention.*** Choose a comfortable, quiet place where you are able to focus without distractions. Take a few deep breaths and remind yourself this is about presence, not perfection.

2. ***Choose materials and notice their textures.*** Take a moment to choose a picture or draw an abstract image. Feel the texture of the paper, and the shape and feel of the pencil in your hand. Abstract images might encourage more focus on coloring, and not on an artistic illustration. Some of my favorite images to color are lots of intersecting circles or a simple flower drawing.

   I use basic coloring pencils. But my friend, Ann, a dedicated coloring practitioner, loves using Prismacolor pencils. Their pigments are more concentrated, and the hues are easy to blend.

3. ***Limit your choices.*** Select just five or six hues to work with. That way you won't spend too much time trying to decide on the perfect colors. Your attention will then be on the coloring process. Having fifty pencil choices might be distracting. But hey, if you love the variety of a large array of colors, go for it. But be sure to use pencils, not markers. Coloring with pencils provides a slower process and allows for shading, depending on the pressure you apply.

4. ***Observe your thoughts.*** Become aware of your thoughts as you color, and refrain from judging your coloring. Be gentle with yourself. If your thoughts wander, acknowledge them and gently let them go. Refocus your attention on the coloring page in front of you, maybe taking note of the movement of your fingers. For a bit of fun and variety, try coloring with your non-dominant hand. Remember to simply continue bringing yourself back to the present each time your mind wanders and refocus on coloring.

Some of us also love to be creative when coloring notecards, or alternatively, handwriting notes, messages, and special occasion cards. As a greeting card company owner and artist for more than forty years, I'm a strong proponent of the handwritten word. When we write a note to someone, we share not only our thoughts and good wishes but a personal artifact—our unique penmanship—as well. A recent study proclaiming the benefits of handwriting for cognition and memory was music to my ears.

DID YOU KNOW?

Norwegian scientists found that handwriting enhances brain connectivity, improving memory formation and helping to encode new information.[155] When we read a text or listen to someone speaking, and then write out the important points by hand or create a diagrammed synopsis, our recall of that information is excellent. Why is this so? Because when writing with pen and paper, the precise hand movements and sensory engagement needed to shape the letters boost neural connectivity in the brain. The more regions of the brain that are involved in learning, the better we retain the new knowledge. In other words, we are engaging our motor control center, so the information becomes more deeply embedded. Handwriting is also a slower process, so our brains engage with the material for a longer length of time, which improves retention. The more time we spend on the information, the more we are able to form connections between ideas. "We show that when writing by hand, brain connectivity patterns are far more elaborate than when typewriting on a keyboard," Professor Audrey van der Meer explained. Typing on a keyboard is good, but pushing letters on a computer is not as effective as handwriting notes for remembering information.

Another curious memory tip came via our son's voice teacher. Jackson was learning several pieces for his operatic and musical performances. During a lesson, Jackson remarked that he was redesigning his bedroom and needed to give it a fresh coat of paint. "Perfect!" said Amy. "While you are painting, sing and practice the lyrics over and over again. Paint and sing, sing and paint, and in no time you'll have those songs committed to memory." A few coats of paint later, Jackson was amazed at how quickly those songs were performance-ready. Why would this be an effective memory strategy? Because, like writing notes by hand, coupling a motor movement with lyrics engages more areas of the brain, allowing for better memory consolidation. Painting walls of a room takes a few hours, so spending this time engaged in memorizing words and music lengthens the period we spend with the material. Then the boredom associated with both memorizing lyrics or painting walls is considerably lessened.

Try This

Grab a card or piece of paper and write a thoughtful, detailed message to someone you appreciate. List why you are grateful for their presence in your life, or why you admire them. I bet every person you know would be thrilled to receive a handwritten letter arriving in their mailbox, acknowledging their goodness. Truth be told, everyone enjoys seeing a real notecard in their mail instead of only bills and advertising flyers.

At their core, all meditation and mindfulness practices anchor us in the here and now, gifting us with a grounded presence and calm awareness. When we practice regularly, we build a foundation of attentiveness that permeates our every action. We live, then, with a balanced spirit that keeps overwhelming stress at bay, fully inhabiting each moment of our lives.

THE GUT-BRAIN CONNECTION

The road to mental health may begin in the gut.

—Dr. David Perlmutter

Have you ever wondered why you feel butterflies in your stomach when you're nervous? This is due to the connection between our mental state and our digestive system. Scientists are discovering many ways that the gut and brain communicate, resulting in both positive and negative effects on our overall health and well-being. This communication runs in both directions, creating a two-way highway between our gut and our brain that is only beginning to be understood.

Entire books have been written on this brain-gut connection, with new studies being published frequently. For example, researchers recently discovered new methods of treating schizophrenia due to the knowledge gained about this relationship.[156] Justin Sonnenburg, PhD, of Stanford is a leading microbiome researcher who calls the gut our second nervous system.[157] It is involved in our overall mental and physical health, influencing anxiety and depression, cognitive functioning, immune system regulation, and how we tolerate stress. Neurological conditions connected to the gut microbiome include ailments such as Parkinson's, Alzheimer's, multiple sclerosis, migraine headaches, autism, and epilepsy.

> *What happens in the gut doesn't stay in the gut.*
>
> —Dr. Emeran Mayer

Dr. Sonnenburg notes that the western diet and lifestyle severely impact the health of our microbiome. We eat too much sugar and too many processed foods, while not ingesting enough fiber or fermented foods. The best diet for nurturing a healthy gut microbiome is the Mediterranean diet, consisting of mostly plant-based foods and healthy fats.

Sugar has a particularly deleterious influence on the gut. It can trigger inflammation, disrupt the microbe balance, lessen the absorption of nutrients due to a more acidic environment, weaken the gut immune system, and disrupt hormone signaling. When I keep this information in mind at the end of the day, that piece of candy looks a lot less tempting.

There are several specific ways the gut influences the brain:[158] First, our gut bacteria produce serotonin, dopamine, and other neurotransmitters, affecting mood and cognitive functioning. Approximately 90 percent of serotonin is produced here. The microbiome helps to regulate our stress, since lactobacillus and bifidobacterium in the gut are associated with lower anxiety and depression scores. Supplementing with probiotics may help reduce symptoms in some cases. Interestingly, some gut bacteria even influence our cortisol levels.

The vagus nerve carries signals from gut bacteria to the brain, influencing mood, stress response, depression, and anxiety. The microbiome also influences the development of the immune system. An unhealthy microbiome can cause inflammation throughout the body and brain, and is associated with diseases such as Alzheimer's and Parkinson's. And, when gut bacteria ferment, short chain fatty acids (SCFAs) are produced, which aid in memory formation and overall brain function.

> *Your mental state can affect your gut health just as much as what you eat.*
>
> —Dr. Robynne Chutkan

Moving in the opposite direction, here's how the brain influences the gut. Chronic stress can alter the makeup of our gut microbiome, causing nausea, digestion issues, diarrhea, and acid reflux, and impact irritable bowel diseases. Our psychological state affects how well nutrients are absorbed and how the gut barrier functions. Trauma can generate a lifelong gut sensitivity, causing myriad physical and psychological issues. If we are stressed, one of the best ways to ensure that nutrients are properly absorbed is to eat mindfully. Focus on each bite, chewing slowly and noticing the subtle flavors of your food. If we are in a positive, relaxed mood when eating, digestion and overall gut health improves.

So we carry a two-lane highway in our bodies, running between the gut and brain, shuttling messages back and forth. This communication is vitally important for sustaining our physical and cognitive health. All the more reason to choose healthy foods as much as possible!

LAUGHTER

A cheerful heart is a good medicine, but a downcast spirit dries up the bones.

—Proverbs 17:22

Another way we can quickly calm our nervous systems, release stress, and boost our happiness is through laughter. Guess how many times most of us laugh per day? Eighteen times! We all enjoy laughing, yet no one knows why. Researchers believe it has been serving important bonding functions between humans since ancient times.[159] When we share a joke or funny story with others, even strangers, we feel closer to them. Even young babies laugh, which strengthens their connection with their caregivers. Most of us laughed more frequently as children than we do as adults, but sharing laughter with others brings a cascade of benefits to all of us. (Of course, laughing at another's expense to humiliate them will not carry the same benefits as innocent, jovial laughter.)

My friend Lisa is a pun aficionado. We roomed together for just one semester in college, when she regularly offered "punny" jokes. Lisa provided much-needed levity as I slogged through my engineering problem sets. We've continued our friendship through the miles and years, with Lisa providing laughs through text messages and memes. Some of her favorite puns are:

How do you properly identify a dogwood tree? *By its bark.*

What do you call a dinosaur that crashes his car? *Tyrannosaurus wrecks.*

Why did the Viking buy a secondhand boat? *He couldn't a fjord a new one.*

I burned my Hawaiian pizza. *I should have used aloha temperature.*

Why don't ants get sick? *Because they have tiny ant-ibodies.*

Why did the hippocampus break up with the amygdala? *Too much emotional baggage.*

> *And in the sweetness of friendship let there be laughter, and sharing of pleasures. For in the dew of little things the heart finds its morning and is refreshed.*
>
> —Kahlil Gibran

I hope a few of those puns made you chuckle, maybe causing you to feel a bit lighter and brighter. Have you ever thought about why laughing like this feels so good? First, it decreases stress hormones like cortisol, which thwart the negative impact of stress on cardiovascular, metabolic, and immune systems over time. Our vulnerability to diseases decreases, since laughing raises the number of antibodies and immune cells in our bodies. Laughter also minimizes your brain's response to threatening situations, so "fight and flight" hormones like cortisol are less likely to be released. Our blood flow and blood vessel function can also improve.

Secondly, the feel-good hormones dopamine and serotonin increase, which promotes relaxation and expands our tolerance for pain. This one-two punch helps to elevate your mood and lessens your physical and emotional response to stress. Laughing also can stimulate the release of oxytocin, which encourages social bonding. Most laughter is shared with at least one other person. If your friend erupts in laughter, you'll likely ask what's so funny and join in the fun.

In one study of couples, people who shared laughter reported "feeling closer to and more supported by their partners."[160]

Lastly, laughter elevates levels of endorphins, which are powerful antidepressants with pain-relieving effects. Writer Norman Cousins used laughter to great advantage when he was battling a painful, life-threatening disease in the mid-1960's. "I made the joyous discovery," he said then, "that ten minutes of genuine belly laughter had an anesthetic effect and would give me at least two hours of pain-free sleep."[161] When hospitals employ clowns to entertain young patients, the children experience less anxiety before their medical procedures.

> *Always laugh when you can. It is cheap medicine.*
>
> —Lord Byron

DID YOU KNOW?

Scientists today find that people who laugh can manage pain longer than people who don't. One study investigated the impact of endorphins in easing pain. (The procedure sounds a bit tortuous, to be honest, so I'm glad I wasn't asked to participate!) The subjects watched humorous videos. Some laughed at them, some did not. Afterwards, the research team strapped an icy cold sleeve over one arm of each person to see how long they could tolerate the cold. The participants who had laughed kept the sleeve on longer.[162] The moral of the story is that if you need to tackle a difficult task, you might want to watch a few funny videos or read a joke book before you begin. But no need to strap on an ice-cold patch!

Across all age groups, laughter helps us cope with the difficulties and challenges of everyday life, and we take ourselves and others less seriously. It boosts our immune systems, improves our sleep, and activates many areas of our brains. When these areas are engaged, the brain can strengthen its neural connections and encourage creativity, problem-solving, and memory.

TRY THIS

It's very easy to find funny videos to instigate laughter: Just head to YouTube and type in the name of your favorite comedian, comedy show, or sitcom. The clips that elicit belly laughs from me are from The Carol Burnett Show, The Mary Tyler Moore Show, I Love Lucy, *and* M*A*S*H *television shows, and clips of routines by Mike Birbiglia and Robin Williams, among others.*

I can't resist telling a funny and embarrassing story from my college days. In the fall of 1976, I was a busy freshman engineering student and athlete at the University of Missouri-Columbia. A few of my volleyball teammates became close friends, and we spent hours together walking to practice, strength training in the gym, and practicing on the court. Long rides to away games provided even more time to nurture our friendships.

Several of us lived in the same seven-story dormitory that housed young men in an adjacent tower, and residents from both dorms shared meals in the dining hall. We often sat with other women athletes, including my roommate, Jill, a breaststroke specialist on the women's swim team. Mealtimes provided rare moments of downtime from our busy schedules when we shared laughter and stories. We had a bit of mischievousness in us, and one evening we concocted a trick to play on Geri, one of the softball players.

Our dining hall provided soft-serve ice cream every day, bestowing a highlight to the otherwise mediocre dormitory food. My friends thought it would be funny if I walked up to the ice cream dispenser with Geri and announced that my ice cream cone smelled bad. We hoped this comment would prompt her to put the cone to her nose, and I would push it into her face—a simple prank that worked according to plan. What happened next, however, was not at all what we had planned or anticipated. Geri laughed loudly, pushing my cone into my face. Somehow that little practical joke turned the entire dining hall into Food Fight Central. The guys began flinging food across tables, even launching bowls of peanut butter through the air. We hid under the tables to escape the barrage of apples, hot dogs, mashed potatoes, hamburger buns, green beans, and every type of food that could be thrown. I'm not sure where the adults were during this mayhem, but eventually a resident assistant appeared and shouted to cease immediately. But the damage had been done; food covered the floor and tables, and the tall window curtains were soiled so badly that they needed to be professionally cleaned. Our little joke, simultaneously funny and shocking, had turned into a scene from *Animal House*. Unfortunately for me, I was blamed for the incident and received a stern warning that if I ever participated in a scene like this again, I would be banned from the dorm complex. I suppose the trouble was worth it, as my longtime friends and I still laugh at the craziness that ensued from that simple prank.

> *The word 'silly' derives from the Greek* selig *meaning 'blessed.' There is something sacred in being able to be silly.*
>
> —Paul Pearsall

One of our daughters sent this joke to our family text chain with my husband, a physics teacher, in mind: A photon is checking into a hotel and the bellboy asks if he can help with the bags. The photon replies, "No need. I'm traveling light." Einstein believed light consisted of particles that came to be called photons. Our family found this to be very funny, and I don't blame you if you think that us finding this funny is pretty funny in itself. To provide a little more laughter for your day, answer this riddle: *What do Winnie the Pooh and Alexander the Great have in common?* (Answer: Their middle name!)

TRY THIS

This week, take a few moments each day to share a joke or funny video with loved ones, in person or virtually. They aren't hard to find these days. Go online and search "funny videos" or "best dad jokes" and you'll be on your way. Your body and brain will thank you.

All of us can enhance our physical and mental well-being through humor.[163] When we share humor with loved ones, we strengthen our relationships and defuse tension. No matter what health issues we might have, the benefits of laughter include improved mood and sleep as well as meaningful reductions in anxiety, depression, stress, pain, and fatigue.[164] With all of those advantages lining up behind laughter, it seems we should *all* find something humorous each and every day.

SMELL

Smell is a potent wizard that transports you across thousands of miles and all the years you have lived.

—Helen Keller

I contracted COVID-19 early in the pandemic, on Monday, March 23, 2020. Three days into my illness, I sat up on the side of my bed to eat a small snack. All of a sudden, without warning, I lost my sense of taste and smell completely. I didn't have any congestion, but I felt a sensation at the bridge of my nose. It wasn't like losing some ability to smell and taste that often accompanies colds. This was a complete and total loss, like a door slamming shut. Instantly, I couldn't taste or smell anything. Little did I know this would be the prevailing side effect of my COVID-19 experience.

I assumed that my taste and smell would return in a few days. I was wrong. Days and weeks passed, and my sadness about not tasting food or detecting smells gave way to fear and anxiety about my safety. I learned just how much we rely on our sense of smell to detect harm. For example, my husband spilled some gasoline in our garage, but I couldn't smell it. A week later, I ate some perfect-looking blackberries that turned out to be rotten, adding a terrible stomachache to my difficulties.

"There must be something I can do to help my senses recover," I muttered to myself, and began researching anosmia, the loss of smell and taste. Several scientists who studied this condition recommended "smell training."[165] Their patients sniffed essential oils for fifteen seconds twice a day, choosing scents from four categories—fruity, flowery, aromatic, and resinous—for twelve weeks. The scientists recommended clove (aromatic) and eucalyptus (resinous), which I had in my essential oil supply. I needed to purchase rose and lemon. Although barely able to walk after four weeks of bedrest, I drove to a nearby store to buy these oils. It was a demoralizing trip. I slowly walked up and down the row of candles and essential oils, struggling to catch a hint of a scent. I found lemon, but needed to find rose oil, or something with its scent, even a spray or candle. But after putting my nose near several products labeled "rose" and inhaling, I couldn't smell anything. Dejected, I resorted to asking a store employee to help me find something that contained a rose scent, confessing that I couldn't detect any scent from the products. Could she tell me which bottle smelled the most like rose? She took the bottles out of my hand, sniffed each one, then confidently announced, "This one is definitely the strongest." I had to take her word for it. My next thought was, "Will it ever return? Is the scent of a rose lost to me forever?"

My ability to smell and taste improved after twelve weeks of training, but it was far from complete. I could make out eucalyptus and clove, but the other two were still unavailable. So, as recommended, I chose a different set of oils from the same categories and continued the training for another twenty-four weeks. The good news is that I did finally and fully regain my taste and smell after about twenty months. (Step-by-step instructions to smell train are here.[166])

Before the pandemic, most of us didn't think much about how we rely on our senses of smell and taste to navigate the world safely. But this temporary loss provided me with a deep appreciation for these senses. (It's crazy how we sometimes need a loss like this to remind us to be grateful for the gifts we enjoy every single day of our lives.) So now I take time to really inhale a variety of scents, including the essential oil products I use to do my cleaning. The assortment of aromas makes these chores quite bearable, if not pleasurable.

Maybe Joan Rivers could have used those scents when doing housework:

> *I hate housework. You make the beds, wash the dishes, do the laundry, and six months later, you have to start all over again.*
>
> —Joan Rivers

As I found out from firsthand experience, our sense of smell impacts our happiness. One of my favorite activities is walking in the woods and enjoying the woodsy scents. I wasn't able to smell anything for months, which brought a sadness to my walks. Scents are often related to memories, too, because the area of the brain where memories are stored is in the same region where we detect scents. Amazingly, our sense of smell begins being developed at three months gestation, when we are bathing in our mother's amniotic fluid, which thereby gives us some tendencies to prefer certain aromas.

Because of the proximity of the brain areas where memories, emotion, and smell reside, when we take in a scent, we feel the emotion first before we can intellectually identify what that smell is. The emotion happens almost instantly, and a millisecond or so later, we realize what memory that aroma evokes. The reason why scents often send us back to childhood memories is that the first imprint we have of a scent and a memory will be what sticks with us over our lifetime. Whatever was happening when we had that initial experience of a smell, that is what comes up in our minds whenever we come across it again. Moreover, that memory is very "sticky," as it takes a lot to dislodge it. So odors that are associated with unique negative experiences, like those that soldiers experience during combat, can be powerful factors in post-traumatic stress disorders. The memory of the odors lingers in their brains; when they appear again, they can trigger the recall of these difficult memories, which can be disabling.

We want to keep our sense of smell intact as much as possible. People who have good olfactory abilities tend to live longer, have better cognitive/mental health, and have stronger social bonds. Lifespan and health span are both intricately connected to the development of a good sense of smell. But when we age, this ability often declines. We can thwart this decrease by noticing various scents throughout the day. Deliberately and mindfully smell various items and think about what they evoke in you. For example, you might smell peanut butter and remember your high school days when you carried a peanut butter sandwich to school every single day. (I'm raising my hand here.) Or perhaps the scent of rose reminds you of your grandmother's rose garden or her perfume. I loved climbing trees in the woods as a little girl and always enjoyed a piney, earthy smell. This scent brings back memories of independence and aliveness. At any rate, pairing a few different smells with recollections will help you foster this important sense.

Unfortunately, smell is discounted by many, including people in the legal profession. In lawsuits where people lose their sense of smell, plaintiffs only receive around five percent of the maximum compensation, whereas if eyesight is lost, it's closer to eighty-five percent.

A study by researchers at University of California, Irvine, showed that nightly aromatherapy improved the cognitive abilities in older adults.[167] The study took place over a six-month period, and standard memory test results were measured. Natural oil diffusers emitted a variety of scents while the participants slept. This exposure lasting two hours nightly led to a remarkable 226 percent increase in cognitive and neural functioning. Incredible, I'd say! The seven scents used in the study were rose, lemon, eucalyptus, orange, rosemary, lavender, and peppermint. They were diffused individually, not combined.

Although the diffuser was used at night, daytime use could work just as well. The researchers say the results confirm what scientists know about the connection between smell and memory. We keep essential oil diffusers in our main living area and our bedroom. My favorite oils are rosemary, lavender, and eucalyptus; I'm hoping they help keep my memory intact for many years to come!

A fascinating fact I recently learned is that we smell not only through our noses but also through the back of our throats. This process is a large part of how we taste and appreciate the food we eat. But we also use our sense of smell when we meet new people; unbeknownst to us, our brains are making judgements about their physiology and psychology. These odors have an impact on our friendships and romantic partners, our emotions, and our hormone levels.

DID YOU KNOW?

Certain diseases can actually be diagnosed simply through analyzing the odors of a person's breath or sweat. Multiple sclerosis, Parkinson's disease, lung cancer, breast cancer, Crohn's disease, diabetes, and melanoma are some of the diseases that can be detected through odors.[168] Researchers can also detect preeclampsia with 84 percent accuracy based on a mother's "breathprint." And the breath of people with diabetes sometimes has a fruity odor.

The human brain is a marvel, constantly being shaped and reshaped by our life experiences and thoughts, our challenges and emotions, and so many other variables. But it is mind-blowing, no pun intended, how we can help mold these changes to our benefit through practices like meditation, healthy eating, coloring, laughter, and other lifestyle choices. This ability to influence our brain's health throughout our lifespan offers all of us hope: We can bring positive change to this vital organ no matter our challenges or circumstances.

PART IV

BONDS

RELATIONSHIPS

I am under the opinion that my life belongs to the whole community and as long as I live, it is my privilege to do for it what I can. Life is no brief candle to me. It is a sort of splendid torch which I have got hold of for the moment and I want to make it burn as brightly as possible before handing it on to future generations.

—George Bernard Shaw

Irish playwright and literary critic George Bernard Shaw was awarded the Nobel Prize for Literature for penning truisms that stand the test of the time. This Shaw-ism is one of my all-time favorite quotes because he summarizes beautifully all the tenets of bonds that I internalized growing up in Catholic schools and communities. And it is true that sometimes we don't even realize the impact of our actions on others until decades later. For example, a few years ago, my ninety-four-year-old father called to ask if I could help him figure out the sender of a birthday card he received. He read the card's message, which expressed gratitude for my dad's friendship and loyalty. As he was reading the words, Dad began choking up and apologized for getting so emotional. In the end, we were able to link the card to a parishioner he had helped through the years. The man's thoughtfulness touched Dad deeply. He said, "I guess, Anne, I did something right along the way." I laughed.

Yes, Mr. Shaw, you are absolutely correct. We are privileged to be here walking on this earth for so brief a time. And yes, it is our responsibility to make the most of our time here, not only to lead fulfilling, productive lives but also that we leave behind a world that is better for the contributions we have made to everyone whose lives we touched. This is not a sentimental notion; this is a deeply profound way to orient our days on planet Earth. Hearing the deep satisfaction my dad felt when he realized he had made a difference in the life of this man proved the point for me once again.

> *Sir, more than kisses, letters mingle souls,*
> *For thus, friends absent speak.*
>
> —John Donne

Let's begin with a simple question: If you could choose just one habit that would have the greatest impact on your health and longevity, what would you select? A better diet, more exercise, higher quality sleep? Of course, each one of these is vitally important, but the most impactful habit is none of those. The most influential, guaranteed-to-improve-your-life strategy for living happily and healthily is to nurture your relationships. Study after study has shown that our connections with others will tip the scales towards health and well-being more than anything else. In fact, having more than 300,000 participants, one of the largest studies confirmed that people with strong social relationships had a 50 percent increase in survival rates compared to people with weaker social ties.[169]

Why do our relationships offer so much protection against deleterious health outcomes? One reason is that friends and loved ones provide buffers to the stressors we face every day. We can discuss our concerns with them and gain support in our difficulties. Our burdens are lightened and our anxieties lessened when we share our struggles with others. These social connections also strengthen our immune systems and help us recover more quickly from illnesses and disease. Studies also show that people with strong relationships have higher self-esteem, are more empathic towards other people, and are more trusting and cooperative. Social connectedness therefore generates a positive feedback loop of social, emotional, and physical well-being.[170]

Social isolation and loneliness negatively impact our health, but each possesses slightly different traits. Social isolation is the absence of social support and connection, which often results in less access to resources that would foster well-being. Loneliness is a subjective state, where people feel alone and disconnected from others, even if they are surrounded by other humans. Loneliness tends to affect mental health and stress responses.

People who are socially isolated experience higher rates of anxiety and depression. They also have a greater chance of suffering from cardiovascular problems, with the risk of stroke increasing by 32 percent.[171] Isolation also causes greater pain sensitivity, more fragmented sleep, accelerated aging, and a decrease in brain function and focus. Feelings of loneliness create alarm bells in our bodies, increasing stress hormones and inflammation.[172] Perhaps the most shocking statistic is that the health effects of loneliness are equivalent to smoking fifteen cigarettes per day, making it twice as unhealthy as obesity.[173] So it's not surprising that being lonely increases the odds of death in any year by 26 percent.[174]

TRY THIS

The former United States Surgeon General, Dr. Vivek Murthy, outlined four steps to keep our connections alive and counteract loneliness. They are:

1. Set aside time every day to reach out to people you love. Just fifteen minutes can increase our sense of connectedness. We don't need to find a new circle of friends. Simply nurture your current relationships.

2. When interacting with people, give them your full attention. "Being fully present," said Murthy, "can make five minutes feel like fifty minutes."

3. Find ways to serve. Service, says Murthy, "reaffirms to ourselves that we have value to add to the world."

4. Nurture silence and solitude, to allow the noise around us to settle and find space to be grateful. This will look different for everyone; for some it could be a walk in nature, for others time spent in prayer or meditation, listening to music, or reading an inspirational text. Moments of quiet time help us reconnect with ourselves and, consequently, to others as well.

> *Perhaps the most important thing we bring to another person is the silence in us, not the sort of silence that is filled with unspoken criticism or hard withdrawal. The sort of silence that is a place of refuge, of rest, of acceptance of someone as they are. We are all hungry for this other silence.*
>
> —Rachel Naomi Remen

When humans are with one another, their bodily systems can begin to align. Our physiology is constantly adjusting to others in ways that are below our conscious awareness. We connect not only through touch but also through mimicry. Mirror neurons in our brains activate when we observe and interact with others, so we may unconsciously mimic the behavior and speaking patterns of other people. Social psychology studies have found that people imitate and mimic others naturally without thinking, and this helps them understand and connect with others emotionally.[175]

DID YOU KNOW?

Scientists see that when subjects are socially excluded, their brains register emotional pain in the very same area of the brain that registers physical pain.[176] These brain areas are known as the dorsal anterior cingulate cortex and the anterior insula. Both are involved in several functions, including emotional regulation and awareness, empathy, decision-making, and time perception. So while physical pain protects us from physical dangers, social pain evolved to protect us from the dangers of isolation. Our brains and bodies are telling us to stay connected to others for our survival and overall well-being.

If I cross my arms, you are more likely to do the same. If I rub my eyes, you are more likely to rub your eyes. We even begin using the same speech patterns as people with whom we're conversing. Laughing and yawning are contagious even among strangers, although the triggers that elicit the mimicking differ between the two. Contagious laughter relies on auditory cues, while yawning mimicry usually relies on visual cues.[177]

Studies show that we are more likely to synchronize movements and gestures with people we feel closest to. Even newborns imitate facial gestures of others just a few hours after birth. One humorous finding is that if someone mimics our movements, we have a better impression of them, even considering them more competent.[178] This can come into play during job interviews; if you know someone who is interviewing for a position, you might want to advise them to mimic the interviewer, as that may increase their chances of landing the job!

When we feel close to a person, our bodies can also become more similar, with our heart and breathing rates often becoming synchronized.[179] The reverse also holds true. When our bodies feel similar, for instance if we are dancing together, walking side-by-side, or playing with a teammate, we feel closer to that person. On the other hand, if we are with someone we don't like very much, our brains and bodies won't synchronize. We expend more effort and energy just to be with them, and this fact explains why some people leave us feeling drained. This knowledge has profound implications for relationships and community building, reminding us to remain patient when in the presence of people who are difficult.

TRY THIS

1. Start noticing how you mimic others, or how they mimic you.
2. When interacting with a challenging person, remind yourself that your body is working a little harder to be understanding and calm. Give yourself some grace.

> *Jewish tradition states that a single visit to someone's sickbed takes away one sixtieth of their illness. Just being in the presence of another human being can lift a person up.*
>
> —Naomi Levy

When I was twenty-seven, I suffered two miscarriages back-to-back. The first happened quite early in my pregnancy, at around six weeks. The second was much more dramatic and heartbreaking. Around seventeen weeks pregnant, I woke up bleeding and cramping. Lying in bed that morning, I was terrified; ultimately, I drove to the doctor's office for a sonogram. Sadly, the pictures failed to show a thriving fetus. I drove myself home, sobbing all the way, and collapsed in my husband's arms on our front porch. Our oldest child Sarah, almost three at the time, remembers that day vividly, with this moment becoming her first memory.

Without my mom or immediate family nearby to lean on, I struggled with this loss. Jack's love and care never wavered, but he was grieving, too. A week or so later, a neighbor called to comfort me and share her experience of miscarriage. Mary Grace's kind words of support as she vulnerably shared her own loss and sadness helped me understand my own feelings and process the heavy pain. Her compassionate presence accompanied me over the next several months, aiding my climb out of despair as I began to embrace life with joy once again. In time, I was pregnant with our second child, elated to add another member to our family.

University of Virginia Professor James Coan studies the neuroscience of emotional and interpersonal behavior. In 2006, his research revealed some remarkable ways our bodies and brains react to pain when in the presence of others, particularly a loved one. He found that holding hands with a married partner helped decrease the brain's threat response to an electrical shock, providing a sense of safety. Because of this effect, the participant was better able to handle the shock, both emotionally and physically. Coan concluded that during medical treatments, the physical presence and touch of a loved one or friend will serve as a gentle pain reliever.[180] Interestingly, for married partners, the buffering effect was proportional to the quality of their relationship. The hormone cortisol is also regulated in some relationships, as with older couples in happy relationships, where the cortisol levels in each other are affected.[181] One partner's positive emotion can cause the other partner's stress levels to decline.

Coan's research shows why we might enlist a friend or family member to accompany us when we are ill or facing painful situations. Their supportive presence, like Mary Grace's, will boost our immune systems and diminish our stress levels. We are then better able to fight off aches and illnesses. Physical touch, affirming words, and calm attitudes have powerful effects on the brains and bodies of those we love. These facts don't surprise me, but I'm thrilled that scientific studies confirm what we have experienced.

PRACTICE

Do you have a friend or family member struggling with a painful experience, or simply going through a rough patch in life? If so, consider reaching out to them to offer gentle support and encouraging words. When you are facing a challenging time, don't forget to share your struggle with people who know you best. More often than not they will be glad you asked for help. We all want to feel needed!

> *There is a lovely balance at the heart of our nature: each of us is utterly unique and yet we live in the most intimate kinship with everyone and everything else.*
>
> —John O'Donohue

I saw a former neighbor at the post office counter one morning and snuck up behind her to give her a big hug. I was so happy to see Donna, as she had been on my mind for several weeks. Her husband was struggling with various health challenges, and it was delightful to see her positive spirit alive and well. We hugged each other several times as she shared some details of her new reality, and we both left the post office with more spring in our steps. Oxytocin, known as the "love" or "feel-good" hormone, increases during positive social interactions like this.

Physical touch can have big benefits for sports teams, as a study on National Basketball Association teams several years ago found.[182] This research was particularly interesting to me because I grew up in a basketball family. We had a half-court in our backyard where neighbors joined us in games, and my dad coached my teams for several years. (He often reminded us before a game, "You can be ladies off the court, but be tigers on the court.") We practiced skills like shooting, passing, and offensive plays, with a heavy emphasis on free throws, which Dad believed was the key to winning games. Unfortunately, back then, none of us knew there was a very simple way of improving performance—and it has nothing to do with skills.

Scientists have seen that physical touch soothes and promotes cooperation and trust. They reasoned that touch would bring about better group play, so they studied professional basketball teams for one year. Their analyses confirmed that "touch predicted improved performance even after accounting for player status, preseason expectations, and early season performance."[183] The teams that gave one another more high fives, and slapped hands and backs more frequently, had better records than teams that rarely did. More touch equaled more wins.

TRY THIS

Think about the teams that you are involved with: work teams, family teams, volunteer groups, etc. Share high-fives, handshakes, and pats on the back, all of which can promote more cooperation, better team unity, and improved outcomes. Of course, only appropriate, consensual touch is recommended.

> *Every time you wake up, ask yourself, "What good things am I going to do today?"*
>
> —Indian proverb

Another robust finding about our connections is that interacting with people we know very little about—even strangers—improves our mood and makes us happier than we would expect. These so-called "weak ties" are important.[184] For example, I chat with Maria, the young woman at our local bakery, when I pick up our bread orders. She recently lost both of her parents and she shared a bit about their lives and how much she loved them. So on my next visit, I gave her one of my sympathy cards, and that small gesture has forged a deeper connection between us.

When I greet checkout clerks by name and ask how their day is going, they are often surprised and delighted to be treated like a real person. These short conversations are so easy to initiate, and they bring light to someone's day even as they improve our own health. Over time, the number of these weak ties more strongly predict well-being than the number of close ties. As researcher Toni Antonucci explains, weak ties "provide you with a low-demand opportunity for interaction" that is both "cognitively stimulating and engaging."[185]

> *Connect deeply with others. Our humanity is the one thing that we all have in common.*
>
> —Melinda Gates

The Dutch, British, and others have used these research findings to offer their citizens opportunities to engage with people categorized as weak ties. The Dutch grocer Jumbo introduced "slow checkouts" for customers, old and young alike, who want to talk with someone. The lines are named *Kletskassa*, which translates to "chat checkout," and patrons are invited to hold leisurely conversations with the store clerk. The program became so successful that the supermarket chain has installed these checkouts in more than one hundred stores. They also added a "chat corner" where locals could meet for a cup of coffee and a chat.[186] Similarly, a supermarket chain in France installed *Blablabla Caisses* lanes, which translates to "blablabla checkouts." (Say that out loud and try not to laugh!) Canadian grocer Sobeys has also installed slow checkout lanes in some of its stores. It seems this feature has caught on in several countries; hopefully, it will become a permanent fixture in fighting loneliness everywhere.

Britain named a Minister of Loneliness in 2018 (as did Japan in 2021). One of the minister's innovations was to install "Chatty Benches," where people are invited to sit and talk, throughout England. The sign on the bench reads, "Happy to Chat Bench. Sit here if you don't mind someone stopping to say hello."[187] These otherwise-typical park benches were introduced to combat loneliness and encourage social interaction, particularly among older people. Other communities around the British Isle quickly picked up on the idea, and it has spread far and wide. Friends who lived in Britain for many years say the culture there is not particularly "chatty," so having a sign like this that invites visits with others is needed.

> *The problem with the world is that we draw the circle of our family too small.*
>
> —Mother Teresa

Slow checkouts and chatty benches can help us forge connections through conversation and attending to one another. These positive interactions with weak ties let our bodies know we are safe, calming our nervous systems. Continue looking for opportunities to reach out to people around you in this way. These efforts will pay off, both for you and your community.

Try This

Who are your weak ties? Take a minute or two and bring them to mind. You may not have a slow checkout line in your grocery store, but perhaps you could pause and ask the clerk how their day is going, maybe even question how long they've been working at the store, or if they have family in the area, or work there full-time.

Tip: Unless it's an emergency, don't talk on the phone or text while you are being waited on. Showing genuine interest in the person in front of you hardly takes a moment but goes far in affirming that they are someone who matters, not just a robot.

SERVICE AND COMPASSION

We are the way light enters the universe.

—Kay Ryan

Last year, a customer called with a special request: Could we gift wrap one of my books, include an assortment of ten cards, and ship the package to her sister-in-law? The recipient was going through some difficult times, and our customer wanted to send a thoughtful, appropriate gift of support and encouragement. Months later, another woman called to order cards printed with messages that would offer affirmation for the incarcerated women she regularly visits. She wanted each woman to receive a meaningful Christmas card in the mail, one that would likely be the only one they would receive.

These generous customers are spreading light to their recipients, bringing solace and a glimpse of joy to people who may not be feeling much of either. The outreach of their actions and ministries, impacting people who are suffering and struggling, is an inspiration.

"Elevation" is the name of the emotion we feel when we witness kind, courageous, generous actions.[188] Levels of oxytocin, the "bonding" or "love" hormone, rise. The increase in oxytocin creates a warm feeling in the heart area and can also inspire a desire to help others.

Elevation—wonderfully—acts as a contagion to spread virtuous actions from one person to another.

Airplanes are one of the small "communities" I frequent, a community in which I occasionally experience this feeling of elevation. One incident took place when I was flying to a conference of religious sisters. I boarded the plane behind two of the sisters, and a young man who introduced himself as Steve jumped up to help them store their luggage. Taking his seat beside the nuns, Steve shared that as a graduate of Catholic schools, he was grateful for the lessons those sisters had taught him. I couldn't help but notice that as more passengers made their way into the cabin, Steve offered his services to anyone needing assistance.

Once we were airborne, Steve and his two new acquaintances seated behind me chatted and laughed for the entire flight. I even heard Steve offer to buy the sisters a drink, which they gladly accepted. I laughed and experienced that marvelous emotion of elevation—and not just because I was 35,000 feet above the ground!

> *Grant me courage to serve others; for in service there is true life.*
>
> —Cesar Chavez

Jack and I were so fortunate to have spent a few hours with Cesar Chavez—a delightful, gentle, humble man—when we drove him to the Pittsburgh airport in the early 1980s. He certainly lived with courage, as he served to secure better wages and working conditions for agricultural laborers. We were quite impressed with his genuine joy and lighthearted presence, as he played with our two-year-old daughter in the back of the car during the drive. He embodied what I have found to be true: The happiest people I know are the ones who are serving others in one form or another. And the variety of roles they play is endless. My circle of friends and acquaintances includes dedicated teachers, accountants, mothers, fathers, hospice volunteers, religious sisters, nurses, doctors, contractors, lawyers, immigration administrators, chefs, and engineers. They may not have the national reach of Cesar Chavez, but they are making meaningful differences throughout their local communities.

The tenth World Happiness Report, released in early 2022, revealed a surprisingly bright light in dark times: Although COVID-19 brought worldwide pain and suffering, it also ushered in increases in social support and benevolence.[189] Global rates of helping strangers, volunteering, and donating increased nearly 25 percent above pre-pandemic levels. It seems that the dominant response to suffering isn't selfishness. It is compassion.

The worst of times often brings out the best in us. Mister Rogers said, "When I was a boy and I would see scary things in the news, my mother would say to me, 'Look for the helpers. You will always find people who are helping.'" When the news of the day overwhelms me (and who among us hasn't felt some of that lately?), I turn to the newsfeeds of the helpers, like the chefs at the World Central Kitchen, who cook for thousands in disaster zones and war-torn areas around the world. I admire their courage, stamina, and compassion, and their adaptable cooking skills that result in vat-sized pots of tasty soups and hearty stews, and sandwiches and dinners, all according to the community and culture. I can barely create a tasty meal like that for one person, let alone thousands, so I cheer in support of them from afar.

> *Releasing, each day, the love that is shackled inside us, and giving it a chance to live. . . . All that matters now is to be kind to each other with all the goodness that is in us.*[190]
>
> —Etty Hillesum

Try This

We cannot possibly help everyone around the globe, but we can do our small part to alleviate suffering where we are. What action can we take today that will lessen the struggles of another person? It may be donating to the courageous World Central Kitchen chefs, but it might also be calling a lonely neighbor to brighten her day. As Mother Teresa reminded us, "We can do small things with great love."

> *In our world full of strangers, we witness a painful search for a hospitable place where life can be lived without fear and where community can be found.*
>
> —Henri Nouwen

Encouraging people who serve is also a way to serve. I received this note from a customer: "I recently sent a card to a family member who is a dedicated clinical nurse. It wasn't anything fancy, just a quick note reminding her of her kind and generous spirit. She responded, saying, 'The card you sent melted my heart. It's so nice to hear positive affirmations, particularly when you haven't heard them much.'" Sometimes we don't realize that expressing our appreciation to people who are doing their part to make the world a better place has value. We never know how much of a powerful impact those few words can have.

> *Love intentionally, extravagantly, unconditionally. The broken world waits in darkness for the light that is you.*
>
> —L.R. Knost

Everybody can be great . . . because anybody can serve. You don't have to have a college degree to serve. You don't have to make your subject and verb agree to serve. You only need a heart full of grace. A soul generated by love.

—Dr. Martin Luther King, Jr.

RITUAL

Rituals give strength and direction to a journey. They are what give meaning to an unpredictable world.

—Tererai Trent

A ritual can smooth life's transition as can perhaps nothing else. . . and serves to intensify appreciation and our joy with celebration.

—Huston Smith

All of us experience a wide variety of rituals, both sacred and secular, fairly regularly. We attend graduation ceremonies, birthday parties, weddings and funerals, and many others, depending on our culture and family traditions. We also perform private, personal rituals, like drinking a cup of coffee in our favorite spot to begin the day, or concluding our day with stretches and an inspirational reading. My husband and I recently hosted a young engaged couple at our home for dinner, where we enjoyed food, stories, and deep conversation. Like many who gather at dinner tables everywhere, we began the festivities by clinking our wine glasses together, saying "cheers" and "salud." This simple toast is a universal ritual, used to commence an evening with friends, or perhaps to celebrate with hundreds at an elaborate wedding reception.

Research shows that these rituals can improve our lives, playing a central role in defining who we are and in maintaining the health of our bodies.[191] Every society across the globe has traditional rituals, so they seem to bring something important to our lives, no matter where we live or what we believe. Our rituals elevate the "ordinary" moments of life and infuse them with a sense of the sacred.

I studied the Hopi Indians of Arizona in graduate school. They believe their rituals help maintain balance and harmony in the world and literally keep this world spinning on its axis. Their ceremonies serve as a vehicle to continue the connection they feel to their ancestors, while ensuring good harvests. Like many cultures, their rituals play a vital role in passing down important traditions, teachings and history.[192]

DID YOU KNOW?

Rituals help us work better by bringing order to our sometimes chaotic lives, giving us confidence and a greater ability to persist. By focusing attention on the elements of the ritual, we tamp down the noise in and around us so we accomplish the necessary tasks. When particular actions carry symbolic meanings, these actions calm us by reducing anxiety and heart rates, and improve our performances.

Rituals help us avoid unhelpful or negative chatter and lower our discomfort. Our prefrontal cortex focuses on the ritual's details, allowing our amygdala to relax. Since rituals are structured, they provide predictability, offering a feeling of control and lessening our anxiety during uncertain times. Some studies find that rituals can calm people as much as anxiety medications. With our attention directed away from our concerns, we are able to forget about them.[193]

Many professional athletes have rituals to calm their nerves and enhance their focus and confidence. They have also been shown to tone down a neural signal associated with performance anxiety and failing.[194] Tennis legend Serena Williams tied her shoes the same way before each match, bounced the ball exactly five times before her first serve, and twice before her second serve. In doing so, she probably felt more able to perform at the high level she needed to win matches. In fact, if she failed to do any of these things and lost, she blamed the loss on the oversight. Another tennis star, Rafael Nadal, perfectly aligned his water bottles in a specific arrangement and direction during matches. This ritual seemed to help him maintain his focus and control on the court. If you doubt that any of these actions can help, remember what we know about placebos: If we think something can help, there's a good chance it will.

Several studies show that coordination of movements promotes bonding, via oxytocin, the "feel-good" hormone. When we move with others, by sitting, standing, kneeling, doing the "wave," or bowing, we perceive ourselves as being more similar—we feel as if we share something in common with the other people in the group, which makes us more likely to have good feelings toward them.[195]

Rituals bind us together, as they did for our ancestors centuries ago. Sharing meals creates intimacy and promotes cooperation with friends. When we participate in a group ritual like a wedding, oxytocin increases in all those people attending. We bond with the other guests, even on the molecular level. How cool is that?

Remarkably, scientists can draw a graph of wedding guests, coded for their proximity to the bride and groom, and the oxytocin levels in their bloodstreams. The graph shows a direct relationship between a wedding guest's connection to the married couple and the amount of increase in their oxytocin levels.[196] People who know the couple well—their parents, best friends, siblings—experience higher levels of oxytocin than people who don't know the couple, such as the "plus one" of a cousin.

> *Intention plus attention turns any activity that we deem worthy into a life-enhancing, sacred act.*
>
> —Fabiana Fondevila

Rituals also have underlying purpose and significance, such as participating in ceremonies with family and friends. My mom and dad's funeral services were highly meaningful for our family and people who attended. These rituals helped us process our loss, share our grief with others, and receive comfort and condolences. In addition, we celebrated our parents' lives and reflected upon the ways they touched all of us during their time on earth.

> *You get awareness of other people's loss, which allows you to connect with that other person, which allows you to love more deeply and to understand what it's like to be a human being.*
>
> —Stephen Colbert

Brazilian researchers studied people who performed rituals and discovered that the rituals were perceived to be more effective depending on their complexity—that is, the number of steps involved, repetition of procedures, and specificity of the proper times to be conducted. The more complex, the more potent they were believed to be.[197]

Why might this be? Our brains tell us that pageantry signals significance, thereby eliciting greater awe. Perhaps you have participated in religious services at Christmas or Easter, where the music, dress, and drama is elevated from a normal service. One of my favorite childhood rituals was attending Tuesday night devotions with my dad. I don't recall all the particulars, but I clearly remember the swinging of the censor, the pungent incense, the candlelight glowing in the darkness, and the solemn repetition of prayers. It was all quite mystical, embedding in me a deep sense of mystery and spirituality.

Some of our rituals occur at sporting events, in which most of us have taken part: standing and singing the national anthem, doing the wave, shouting your team's cheer with the crowd, or waving the Terrible Towels, as they do at Pittsburgh Steelers games. My husband and I are alumni of Penn State University, known for its rabid football fans and its exceedingly large Beaver Stadium, the second-largest college football stadium in the U.S., with more than 106,000 seats. My favorite part of a football game there is participating in the ritual of singing Neil Diamond's "Sweet Caroline" in the third quarter. I recorded the crowd belting out the song, and I shook my fists with everyone else when the "bum bum bum" part was sung. (The student section shakes their pom poms to the three beats.) I'm sure everyone there feels happier at the end of the song. What a great ritual!

One of the most exciting rituals I've personally witnessed took place years ago, when my husband and I visited Siena, Italy, during the running of the Palio. This wild horse race, initiated in its modern form in 1633, is held twice a year in the summer, pitting the neighborhoods of Siena against one another. On the eve of the race, we attended the historical parade that featured participants in medieval costumes, chariots, horses, drummers, and flag-throwers. The next day, horses and riders representing each *contrada*, or city ward, zoom around the central piazza three times, with thousands of spectators cheering them on. The winning horse does not even need to have its rider atop in order to win, so the jockeys often attempt to knock one another off their horses, hoping to slow the rival horses. Jack and I were able to stand inside the track and watch this crazy competition, which I described as the Super Bowl of ancient horse racing, up close. The cheers were deafening, and we were gladly swept up in the excitement.

A victory in the Palio is a source of pride for the winning *contrada*, and the triumphant neighborhood hosts an all-night party in celebration. Our accommodations, a bedroom in Catherine of Siena's convent, happened to be in the *Oca* (Goose) *contrada*, which won the race the day we attended. We didn't sleep much that night, since the revelry below our window carried on until dawn. However, experiencing this ancient ritual up close provided a glimpse into Siena's history, culture, and communal celebrations. We will never forget being a part of it, either!

TRY THIS

Bring to mind rituals that you participate in, whether at sporting events, religious ceremonies, or family gatherings. What elements do you most enjoy? Can you list several ways that the ritual(s) impacts you, both immediately and long-term? Recall rituals in which you participated in the past, or ones you're curious about. What purpose do they serve, and would you benefit from taking part in any of them now?

Here's a short ritual you can do by yourself or with a group: Cross your arms over your heart, like you are giving yourself a hug. Or you can cup your cheeks with your hands. Now choose one of these pairs to recite and close your eyes:

Inhale: "I breathe in (God's) Love."

Exhale: "I rest in (God's) Peace."

Or,

Inhale: "Breathing in peace."

Exhale: "Letting go of worry."

Children as young as two years old have already internalized the meaning of rituals like birthday celebrations. Research shows that young children believe that the reason why people get older is that they are given a birthday party.[198] When guests sing "Happy Birthday," someone blows out the candles on a decorated cake, and everyone eats a piece of the cake—maybe topping it off with a scoop of ice cream—then and only then do you advance one year. Young children believe that if you don't have a party, you don't turn a year older. Looks like we discovered the fountain of youth: Don't have birthday parties!

Sometimes rituals are simple, solitary ones. When I get stuck while preparing a talk or writing an article, I often head to our kitchen and begin wiping countertops, washing plates and utensils, or rubbing spots off the floor, anything to take my mind off the task at hand. I let my mind wander and focus on spraying the cleaning product, taking in its scent, and watching dirt and grime disappear. After several minutes of polishing and scrubbing, I'm ready to return to my work with a clearer head. This cleaning ritual serves as a "reset" button for my creativity and motivation, leaving me with a small sense of accomplishment and a sparkling kitchen.

The point is that when we are feeling anxious or stressed, scientists tell us to create a ritual. Invite friends to share a meal, sing together, or play a few board games. The experiences will allow us to transcend our solitariness and deepen our experience of life. We can all toast to that!

MOVEMENT

The very fact of congregating is an exceptionally powerful stimulant. Once individuals are gathered together, a sort of electricity is generated.

—Émile Durkheim

I recently attended an aerobic dance class at our local YMCA for the first time. One motivation for attempting a novel class is that I knew it would be a great workout for my brain. Trying unfamiliar dance steps would challenge my concentration, and I'd meet new people while enjoying a different form of exercise. However, I did not anticipate just how friendly and helpful my classmates would be.

I arrived early to stake out a spot at the very back of the room. As soon as I set my bag down, one of the class members introduced herself and informed me that the back sometimes becomes the front. Since my dance abilities are almost nonexistent, I quickly repositioned myself. Several other women then approached me to offer words of encouragement, as they could see I was a newbie. Class began, and I struggled to learn the steps and obviously looked discombobulated. Mid-class, one of the regulars walked over to me and whispered a few tips in my ear. I was touched by her kindness and care, and tried to readjust based on her advice. At the end of class, many congratulated me for my efforts, clumsy as they were. I walked out of the Y feeling happy and supported. My brain and body had a workout, but my heart was full of joy.

The renowned sociologist Émile Durkheim coined the phrase "collective effervescence" to describe the feeling we often experience when moving with others. We might be dancing in a class like this, walking in a fundraiser with others, or swaying and singing in church or at a sporting event. Whatever form they take, these activities help us to feel connected to one another and allow us to transcend our individual lives. I definitely felt more connected to the women I met that day and can't wait to try the dance class again.

Kelly McGonigal, PhD, who researches group movement, finds that exercising with others is particularly helpful to our health and well-being.[199] She says that exercise is not just about being physically fit. Moving with others is a particularly powerful way to reduce stress and nurture joy, connection, and a sense of belonging. McGonigal reveals that sharing physical challenges, like all of us attempting to follow an instructor's intricate dance moves, creates strong social bonds and increases cooperation and trust among participants. We are bound together by our "collective effervescence." And due to the increase in oxytocin, that bonding and feel-good hormone in our bloodstreams, we may become more empathic and socially aware. So you might want to say *yes* to the next opportunity to walk with others, join an exercise class, or dance at a gathering. You'll be glad you did!

I grew up playing a variety of sports, mostly with my older brother and his friends. My parents valued the lessons we could learn from teamwork, even when opportunities for young girls weren't readily available. In the spring of 1972, I'd recently graduated from St. Dominic Savio Grade School and would be entering Notre Dame High School in the fall. As a basketball player coached by my dad, I wanted to continue improving my skills. So in early June, I was excited to read a notice in the St. Louis South County Journal about a weeklong basketball camp at Affton High School, the local public school. In the early 1970s, sports camps for girls were nonexistent. None. Not a single one—which seemed unfair and very disappointing. So I scanned the tiny two-inch by one-inch basketball camp announcement and realized it did not explicitly state that the camp was open to "boys only." I immediately told my mom and dad that I wanted to sign up. Mom chauffeured me to the athletic office. We walked in the door and told the secretary we were there to fill out the basketball camp forms. She shook her head and said, "I'm sorry. This camp is for boys only." With mom standing by, I showed the secretary the clipping and pointed out it did not indicate that girls were not allowed. The secretary shrugged, handed us the enrollment papers, and I took part in the camp a few weeks later. I was the only girl and wasn't the worst player there, thank goodness. Almost, but not quite.

Unbeknownst to me, my dad had called Affton's head basketball coach, a man he knew through coaching, before the first day of camp to let him know that I would be attending. He didn't ask if it was okay; Dad just simply told him I was coming, adding, "I have one request, coach. When you play 'Shirts and Skins' during the scrimmages, please assign Anne to the 'Shirts' team." And he did. ("Shirts and Skins" is a common method for dividing players into two easily distinguishable teams for pickup basketball games. One team, the "Shirts," keeps their shirts on, while the other team, the "Skins," takes their shirts off and plays bare-chested. It's an easy way to keep track of each team when uniforms aren't available. Obviously, being on the "Skins" team would have been mortifying.)

Sometimes we need to take risks in order to make new connections. It's not always comfortable to invite a new acquaintance to take a walk in the park or sip a cup of coffee with us. We may need a bit of courage to join a group of unfamiliar people in a pottery class. But we can recognize the opportunity to make new friends and learn different skills, however uneasy we might feel in taking that first step. Remembering to bring along our sense of humor always helps to dampen any misgivings we might be holding. Our bodies and minds will thank us!

Somehow connect with someone who you think of as a treasure in your life, someone that illuminates your life, who reminds you of the power of love and the remembrance of radiance. Reach out and affirm what keeps saving us—goodness, kindness, faithfulness, gratitude, generosity, hospitality, justice and love. . . always love. Lay your hand on your heart and know that you also illuminate the lives of others around you. You are also doing what you can each day, in your own way, to make the world around you a kinder place.

—Carrie Newcomer

All of us, at some time or other, need help. Whether we're giving or receiving help, each one of us has something valuable to bring to this world. That's one of the things that connects us as neighbors—in our own way, each one of us is a giver and a receiver.

—Mister Rogers

SINGING TOGETHER

Choral music goes to the very heart of our humanity, our sense of community, and our souls.

—John Rutter

Singing in choirs is a community-building activity that provides one of the most effective ways to boost our overall health and well-being. Singing holds a very special place in my heart because that's how I met my husband, Jack. As members of a folk group in college, we fell in love over the course of a semester, singing and playing our guitars next to each other. Little did I know then of the health benefits of singing with others.

How exactly does singing nurture our well-being? Learning new songs stimulates our brains, boosting our memory abilities. When we sit up tall and regulate our breathing while singing, we improve our posture and our muscles. Singing also helps reduce cortisol and increases an important antibody known as immunoglobulin A (IgA).[200]

Have you ever noticed that when you sing with others, you just feel better? Even if you can't, as the saying goes, hold a tune in a bucket, you probably get a lift just by trying. Why? Because the feel-good hormones like endorphins, dopamine, and serotonin increase, and our sense of social closeness with others elevates our moods. Although simply listening to music can help relieve pain, people feel more positive emotions after actively singing than when they passively listen to music. And singing is one of the quickest ways to feel connected to people we don't know.[201]

> *I don't sing because I'm happy. I'm happy because I sing.*
>
> —WILLIAM JAMES

No matter your age, you might want to sing with others every chance you can. "Music may have emerged during the evolution of human species to promote social interaction and sense of community by synchronizing the bodies and emotions of the listeners," says research fellow Vesa Putkinen of the Turku PET Centre in Finland.[202] For older adults, the health benefits of singing together are numerous. Studies show participants have fewer falls and doctor visits, and less need for prescription drugs. Older singers maintain better social connections and cognitive function, even helping people suffering from dementia.

My dad was a funny guy and a regular warbler. Whenever "How Great Thou Art" was sung at Mass, he would come home singing it full-throated, continuing his solo concert as he walked around the house or made breakfast. Many times he'd change the words to "How Great I Am," laughing and saying, "You all *must* sing that song at my funeral!"

I got the call as I was waiting to board my flight to St. Louis: My dad had contracted pneumonia a few days before, and, at ninety-four, his body could no longer fight the infection. My siblings were keeping watch at his bedside; my sister assured me that she had told Dad several times that I was on my way. Even though I didn't make it there to tell him goodbye, he knew I was coming, and that knowledge was comforting to me. My mom had passed away just ten months prior, and she and Dad never spent a wedding anniversary apart. They both outlived all their siblings, so we were very conscious of the gifts of years we had with them. Our family was also truly grateful that in their last days, neither suffered for very long.

I volunteered to plan Dad's funeral and celebration of life. It was an easy task, since Mom had left us instructions, in her elegant "old-timey" handwriting, on what songs were to be sung, where to hold the reception, what priest should preside, and other arrangements. But, for me, the easiest part of planning Dad's funeral was choosing the recessional song.

Of course, with tears and laughter mixed together, we sang "How Great Thou Art" as we processed out of church at the conclusion of my father's funeral. I explained to the church organist why some of us might be laughing as we sang, as our dad would be providing us one last moment of merriment.

Try This

If you have a spot in your schedule for singing with a group, find one in your community. It could be a church choir, a glee club, or leading songs at a local nursing home. Or simply cue some familiar songs and invite family members to join in.

Who knew that singing with others could be so uplifting for body and mind? Be on the lookout for opportunities to sing and savor the camaraderie and bonds that develop.

KINDNESS AND CONNECTIONS

To have joy, one must share it.

—Lord Byron

On the morning of December 22, my husband and I were preparing to fly to San Francisco to spend the Christmas holiday with our son and daughter-in-law. A few hours before we departed for the airport, I received a call from a customer named Judy. She needed three packs of New Year's cards and was hoping to receive them quickly. I asked, "Where do you live?" If she lived on the East Coast, I was certain she would have them in a few days. But her answer—Berkeley, California—made me smile. "I'm heading to your area in a few hours and could tuck the cards into my backpack. You can pick them up at our hotel, if that's convenient." "Of course," she said, "That would be perfect." So I packaged up the cards and left them at the hotel's front desk when we arrived.

However, Saturday afternoon's traffic was more than Judy wanted to tackle. She called and asked if her sister, who lives near the hotel, could pick up the cards. "Sure," I said. "What street does she live on?" When she replied, "Carl Street," I started smiling. "And what might be her address?" I asked. Her response turned my smile into a loud chuckle. "She lives right next door to our son!" I exclaimed. "I'll hand deliver them within the hour." I met Judy's sister soon after.

All day long, I couldn't wipe the smile off my face or stop retelling the story to anyone who would listen. We *all* love "small world" stories, don't we? They remind us how connected we are, and that realization can't help but bring us joy.

> *I see letters I have received as sacraments, holy things, paper tabernacles that contain the love of my friends.*
>
> —Edward Hays

Scientist Neil Theise reminds us of how connected we are biologically, even down to the molecular level.[203] We send molecules out from our bodies in a few ways, including via exhalations and sweat. We take in molecules through eating, breathing, and skin absorption. This means that there is a constant molecular exchange going on between us and our environment, without a clear boundary between the molecules that are ours and those that exist outside our bodies. This continual exchange of molecules with the world around us creates an ongoing connection with the planet's entire biomass.

On the same trip to San Francisco, I overheard a conversation between two men in the hotel breakfast area. "My daughter moved here at the end of the pandemic to be close to her employer instead of working remotely from the East Coast. But she was disappointed to find that many of her co-workers were still working from home." The man's daughter was struggling with isolation, and didn't have a group of friends with whom she could socialize. It was a familiar story of loneliness and disconnection.

In the United States, we laud young people who move far away to pursue their careers, but they do so at what cost to their mental well-being? Are they leaving the very support systems and connections that allowed them to dream big, only to discover that those supports are essential to their happiness and well-being? I am not suggesting that we discourage young people from pursuing their goals and ambitions. But we need to keep in mind that relationships are essential to our ability to thrive and be happy.

> *Can we expand our vision of community beyond our own skin, family, race, tribe, culture, country, and species? Spiritual life is more than what we believe, it also includes how we relate. Who is included in the 'we' and who is not? That is both a spiritual and a political question. How we answer it will likely determine our future.*
>
> —Jim Wallis

A small card order placed by one of my customers, a sweet lady named Helen, was seemingly lost in the mail. We sent a second package and asked her to return the first one if it ever arrived. A few days after mailing the second package, we received this note from Helen:

> Well, I found out what happened to the first package of cards. While walking my dogs over the weekend, I ran into an older woman who lives on our street. Let's just say she's not the easiest to get along with. I was puzzled when she approached me and proceeded to thank me for the cards I sent her. I asked her to refresh my memory and wondered if they were Cards by Anne. "Yes," she said, "and they're lovely! Thank you! I will really enjoy them." That was the most pleasant experience I've ever had with this woman. I didn't have the heart to tell her that was not my intent. She seemed so pleased that I was not going to take that away from her, especially when I've experienced very little joy from her.

This small act of kindness, accidental though it was, brought Helen's neighbor unexpected joy. It's a good reminder, cliche or not, that little things can make a big difference. It's also a reminder that sometimes the people who seem least deserving of our love, ill-tempered due perhaps to illness or loneliness, are the ones most in need of it.

One of the lessons we've learned from our ongoing experiment with technology's side effects is that face-to-face interactions build stronger social connections and life satisfaction compared to interactions via social media and text messaging. Researchers have also found that in-person, reciprocal relations lead to lower depressive symptoms. This is not to suggest that we need to become party animals! Socializing at least weekly or monthly provided better health outcomes, with no added benefits associated with socializing more frequently.[204]

TRY THIS

Call a friend and set up a time to take a walk, grab a cup of coffee, or catch a movie together. We need each other!

> *Every single one of us has a good work to do in life. This good work not only accomplishes something needed in the world, but completes something in us.*
>
> —Elizabeth O'Connor

It was late May 2022. My siblings and I arrived at Seven Holy Founders church to set up flowers and pictures for my mom's funeral. Our dad would arrive a bit later. All the participants from the early morning Mass had departed the church except for one elderly man sitting in the pew. None of us knew who he was, so we approached to let him know a funeral would be taking place within the hour. He said, "Yes, I know. I'm here to support your dad." He and my dad were teenagers in the early 1940s, living on the same street in St. Louis. This gentleman hadn't seen our dad in eight decades, and yet he came to offer his condolences. When we asked why he had gone to such lengths to be there, he explained that Dad had helped him get a job when his father became ill and his family was struggling financially. When Dad mentioned to his manager at the drugstore that this other boy needed work, the boy was hired. That long-ago act of kindness helped his family survive, and he never forgot it.

This amazing story reminded me of a recent study that explored whether people realize the impact of a small act of kindness on the recipient. The research, conducted by Amit Kumar of the University of Texas at Austin and Nicholas Epley of the University of Chicago, showed that kind people usually underestimate the value of their acts of kindness and how much happiness those acts bring the recipients.[205] And it didn't seem to matter what type of kindness they offered, how big it was, or whether it involved an action taken or a material gift. It didn't even matter if the recipient was known by the giver. Kind people were always off in their predictions of how greatly their gesture meant to the recipients. In other words, random acts of kindness have an outsized ability to boost our happiness as well as the happiness of the recipients.

When I asked Dad about his long-ago kind action, he replied, "I don't even remember doing that."

Try This

Small gestures of kindness and generosity can make a big difference in another's life, and will boost your happiness, too. Here are a few suggestions to practice kindness:

1. Invite another shopper to go ahead of you at the grocery store.
2. Bring a small bouquet of flowers to an elderly friend.
3. Share homemade cookies with your mail carrier or sanitation worker.
4. Send a card to someone who is struggling or could use a bit of affirmation.
5. Give a sincere compliment to a stranger. Do they have a nice smile, a great hat, a cute dog?
6. Find something nice to say to someone at least once a day.

Early one morning, while waiting curbside at the Pittsburgh airport, I witnessed the older woman ahead of me give a long hug to her niece as they parted, each saying, "I love you" more than once. I gently inquired about where she was headed and what brought her to Pittsburgh, which sparked a lovely conversation. As the line moved forward, my new friend took a wobbly step and dropped her coin purse, scattering change all over the sidewalk. I jumped ahead of her and began picking up the coins, since she was unable to bend over and gather them herself. I was on the ground for no more than thirty seconds, but the woman thanked me profusely, saying, "Thank you so much for your kindness! It was so nice of you to help!" as though I had performed some extraordinary act.

I am certain that every one of you reading this could tell a similar story about a simple act of kindness you performed. We know just how little it takes to brighten someone else's day. We have so much power and agency to affect others. But how often do we think about what that action does for us? As for me, I know that my heart was filled with joy because I was able to help someone, and it meant so much to her that I did.

All of us would agree that kindness is an important virtue, one that we want to practice regularly. But we don't always do so. What keeps us from acting on this belief? Author Houston Kraft notes three reasons why we might bypass an opportunity to be kind:[206]

1. **Incompetence:** We may believe we don't have the particular skill needed to perform the act of kindness.

2. **Insecurity:** We worry that the compassionate act we are considering will be met with judgment, dismissal, or even laughter.

3. **Inconvenience:** We are simply too busy, too tired, too overwhelmed, with a mind too full of things to do. We just don't think we have the time to do the kind thing.

All of these excuses begin with the same letter, "I," which is (not surprisingly) also the source of our biggest obstacle. I have found that if I take the risk, my action is nearly always met with appreciation—often effusive appreciation—that indicates what I did meant a great deal at the same time as it really warmed my heart. Don't second-guess your kind act! Just *do* it!

> *Lesson of the moment: I am not a little autonomous being, deciding this or that about my own life without interference. I am a thread in a tapestry of people.*
>
> —Deborah Good

A *tapestry of people.* What a lovely image to encapsulate our circle of friends, colleagues, relatives, and loved ones. The pandemic years brought losses to so many of us. My parents died within ten months of each other, although not from the virus. Neither had terminal illnesses, but they were both in their nineties, and so we knew they were living on borrowed time. I visited them a few times each year, and on an early April weekend, I assisted my mom in making dinner for my dad. She was cutting onions and pressing hamburger patties with her small hands, complaining a bit about how much they hurt. But we were laughing and enjoying the simple task of preparing food together. Little did I know that three weeks later, Mom would be in the hospital and receiving a diagnosis of an aggressive blood cancer. The doctors gave her a few weeks to live. I was stunned. How could the woman I was recently chopping onions with have only weeks to live?

But Mom, being a retired nurse, took her diagnosis with stoicism and gratitude. She then taught us a beautiful lesson in how to die with grace and gratefulness. She spent those few weeks in pain, but with a deep sense of appreciation for the long life she enjoyed, and of the time she had been given to say goodbye to all of us. Many of us traveled to St. Louis to be with her in her final days; some were only able to visit via Zoom. What a gift to be able to feed her ice chips while listening to her express heartfelt gratitude for having time to say goodbye to people closest to her! She died on May 2.

When we lose more than a few threads in our personal tapestry of people, it is to be expected that we will feel adrift. For me, what once were the routine joys of life became big, gaping holes: *Who will I call to share good news about our kids and grandkids, now that my mom is gone? It feels too much like boasting when shared with friends or other family members.* I regularly called my mom during my frequent drives or flights to weekend retreats or conferences. Unfailingly, she would ask, “So where *are* you right now? And where are you *going*?” This was so much a part of our relationship, I actually posed the question to her as she was dying. "Who will I call?" I asked, and then told her how much I was going to miss all of our "catch-up" conversations. Without even opening her eyes, and in her typical no-nonsense, unsentimental way, she said, "Call your sister." When our son called her via Zoom, she concluded the call by saying, "Have a great life, Jackson, and keep being a good person."

Whew. Tears welled up in my eyes as I heard those words, a final blessing of sorts to Jackson from my mom. Those last moments were a treasure, a rich and poignant experience, as we shared Mom's last days on earth.

TRY THIS

Think of a difficult time in your life. Now try to recall something you learned or experienced during that time, something for which you are grateful.

While watching the 2022 Winter Olympics, I witnessed a scene that stopped me in my tracks: A United States snowboarder, poised to win a gold medal with just one competitor remaining, cheered on the final snowboarder's run and then jumped up with glee and hugged the New Zealand woman who had just beaten her out of the top prize. I could scarcely believe my eyes. Did we really see an Olympic competitor's full-throated joy for the success of her challenger? I was both shocked and moved. These young athletes demonstrated to the world what true community looks like. They were honestly happy for and celebrated one another's success, even if that success meant the disappointment of their own hopes and dreams.

For many spring seasons, we watched mama robins build nests in the rafters and lay eggs just outside the large windows at Cards by Anne. We were treated to the lightning-fast, wondrous growth of baby birds: skinny, featherless creatures, mouths wide open begging for food, transformed almost overnight into full-feathered fledglings, practicing flying. Until, boom! Away they go!

Last spring, however, as I peered out the windows to gauge "our" little birds' progress, I was brokenhearted to see that the rafters were totally clear. Not even a stick remained. My mind was confused. I couldn't imagine what had happened. The location is too protected for wind to have caused such complete destruction. The only reasonable conclusion was that a predator had grabbed the nests, baby birds and all.

Ornithologist Kaeli Swift advises the "broken-hearted nest observer" that "predation is the transfer of life and that life is a gift. It's a gift that ensures the survival of another, and even if we don't know that individual as well as the one we watched perish, it's not for us to assert that it, or its offspring, deserves that gift any less."[207] Ok, I thought. I'll keep that in mind. Swift offers sage advice that we can apply to human societies as much as to wildlife: We should allow ourselves to feel deeply for the wildlife around us, and teach our children and friends and neighbors to do the same. We can learn empathy and caring from nature, and we will discover in this experience how to think about the community—not just the individual—first and foremost.

TRY THIS

Take time this week to observe birds in your neck of the woods. One of the best ways to get to know your neighborhood feathered friends is to download the Merlin app on your phone. It will identify birdsong in your area so you can delight in their songs every day. But I must warn you that this app can be addictive!

In what ways do you strengthen your connections with neighbors, colleagues, acquaintances? Continue exploring ways to expand and nourish the tapestry of people in your life. By nurturing those bonds and relationships, you will boost everyone's joy and happiness.

BODY BUDGETS

I think we need a new word, 'comjoyment,' as a companion to 'compassion' to remind us that our greatest gift to the world may be in sharing what gives us the greatest joy.

—Sam Keen

A few years ago, we spent the week with three of our grandchildren and their parents, enjoying activities that occasionally teach a life lesson. (Besides the lesson that I'm no longer twenty-five years old!) Seven-year-old Percy, five-year-old Sawyer, and I went to the dollar store to buy a few art supplies, natch. We wound up also buying a remote-control helicopter, because Numa couldn't say "No." Arriving home, Sawyer ran outside to launch it in the air. It flew for about fifteen seconds, then crashed to the ground. Repeating this over and over again, Sawyer squealed with delight. But after a while, she turned to me and said, "I need Percy to come out and see this!" She ran toward the house, yelling, "Percy! You need to come here!" They returned together and Sawyer handed the controller to Percy. She screamed with joy as he launched the helicopter above them. Her happiness was now complete, since her big brother was there to enjoy the helicopter flying with her.

When I mentioned this episode to our daughter Elizabeth, she said Sawyer always wants Percy to be nearby when she is having fun. Of course, like most siblings, they fight like cats and dogs occasionally. But I was reminded of how much our joy is magnified when we can share it with others, a lesson we learned during COVID-19 lockdowns. Savoring moments of joy with loved ones makes good times some of the best times.

> *"There may be no dissension within the body, but the members may have the same care for one another. If one member suffers, all suffer together with it; if one member is honored, all rejoice together with it."*
>
> —1 Corinthians 12:25–26[208]

There are reasons why it is true that all parts work together, suffer together, and celebrate together—even down to the molecular level. Lisa Feldman Barrett, PhD, is a neuroscientist who studies how we regulate one another's "body budgets." She defines body budgets as the way we manage our body's energy needs and stores. The brain's main job, she notes, is not to think, but rather it is to maintain our bodies' functions so we can breathe and eat and move and survive.[209] Imagine the brain as an accountant for our overall existence, tallying up what is needed, tracking what resources are available, and anticipating how our bodies are going to respond to those needs.

We affect one another's bodies and nervous systems through our words and actions. We probably intuit this fact already, but scientific tools now allow us to see what's taking place in our brains. The brain regions that process language overlap significantly with those that regulate vital bodily functions. This network helps maintain our major organs and heart rates, adjusts levels of glucose in our bloodstream, and regulates the flow of chemicals that support immunity.[210] Amazingly, the words we hear and speak influence the bodies of other people, directly affecting brain activity and physical systems.

This means that I can increase your body budget or decrease it, depending on my actions. If I raise my voice at you, your heart rate and the hormones in your bloodstream will be affected, depleting resources from your body budget. If I criticize you continually, your brain and body will be physically injured. Conversely, if I regularly compliment you, your body budget will increase. This is one reason why people in loving relationships get sick less often and usually live longer than people who are lonely. Their bodies are being nourished by the positive, loving comments and actions of their loved ones. And if they do get seriously ill, they are more likely to recover.

Our facial expressions and actions affect others; if we are in a stressful situation and are anxious, nervous, or overwhelmed, our attitude affects the people around us. We know this from experience, don't we? Our stress affects the brains and bodies of each person we engage with. Their interactions with you, and your interactions with them, will tune and prune the neurons of your brains. Every day, microscopic parts of your brain are changing as you interact with others.

The Harvard Study of Adult Development, running eighty-five years now, concluded that the key to living longer can be boiled down to one thing: loving relationships.[211] Everyone around us, then, friends, family members, even strangers, contribute to, or subtract from, our body's energy needs. Knowing about this remarkable research, I more readily offer words of affirmation and encouragement, even to strangers. If I think a pleasant thought about someone, I don't hold it inside. Perhaps we should all be wearing capes, since we possess superpowers to help and affect every person we encounter. When I chat with the lady in the bakery, I comment on her delicious offerings. I say "Good morning!" to the neighbor's landscapers, oftentimes in my limited Spanish, and tell them what a great job they are doing. My words may be the only positive affirmations they hear all day, and I feel better as a result, too. People often feel happier offering kindness than receiving it, and that happiness tends to linger for a long time.

TRY THIS

This week, notice the good in the people around you—and tell them!

> *I am overwhelmed sometimes and feel a great deal of wonder at words, just simple words and how deeply we can touch each other with them.*
>
> —Leslie Marmom Silko

Indeed, words can touch us deeply. Recently I received two beautiful thank you notes from customers, which brightened my day and brought an extra spring to my step. When we send thoughts of love, support, and encouragement, whether on a greeting card (my favorite medium, of course!), in a text, or via a phone call, our simple messages can comfort, affirm, and deepen our connections with people we care about. Isn't that what life is all about?

As Dr. Barrett tells us, "The best thing for your nervous system is another human and the worst thing for your nervous system is another human."[212] When we treat one another with simple kindness, there is a real biological benefit. Maybe that's why I felt I had a little bit more energy after reading those affirming words from customers! When we have empathy for another person, our brain predicts what they'll think, feel, and do. The more familiar people are, the more efficiently our brain predicts their inner thoughts, feelings, and struggles. This process feels natural to us, as though we are reading another's mind.

But when people are less familiar, it can be harder to empathize. Our bodies and brains will expend more energy during an encounter with people from other cultures and backgrounds because it's metabolically costly for our brains to deal with people who are difficult to predict. Our brains use more resources when figuring out what a stranger is thinking, feeling, and doing. It's just easier, and less tiring, to be with people we agree with and who share our worldview. This knowledge helps us understand that exercising the "muscles" of empathy and compassion will take more effort when we engage with individuals whose language, beliefs, or customs are very different from ours. Similarly, people create online echo chambers because it's less costly to their body budgets. It's far easier, mentally and physically, to surround ourselves with views that reinforce our beliefs. Being aware of these energetic expenses helps us nurture patience with ourselves as we prepare for these more tiring conversations. We're also better at our jobs if we are working with others we know and trust. Our body budgets aren't burdened, so we have more resources to be creative and solve problems. Tech companies provide free lunches, in part, to foster relationships, and as a byproduct, more creativity.

> *Walk cheerfully over the world, answering that of God in everyone.*
>
> —George Fox

George Fox's advice strikes me as timely and appropriate, even though it was offered several centuries ago. Fox's counsel did not originate from an idyllic era, as he lived in a time of social upheaval and war—not so different from our times. We certainly see pain and struggle all around us today. But I would argue that "walking cheerfully" throughout our everyday encounters may be more important now than ever before. Even the smallest of actions can lead to outsized effects on others. As Dr. Barrett reminds us: "There is a real biological benefit when people treat one another with basic human dignity. We are free to speak and act, but we are not free from the consequences of what we say and do."[213]

When we treat each person we meet with the belief that they are a valued member of the human community, we send a clear message that they matter and that their presence is acknowledged and appreciated. We have enormous influence to positively affect people around us. Mr. Fox did not know back in the 1600s that a kind word or compassionate gesture can actually change a person's heart rate, blood pressure, bloodstream chemicals, and brain. But he would agree that these invisible ripples of human connection strengthen not only individuals, but entire communities.

TRY THIS

Here are a few simple suggestions to boost the people you encounter:

1. If you can do so safely, make space for another driver and wave them into your lane during rush hour.
2. Check in on a friend or neighbor who recently lost a loved one.
3. Grow your immediate circle by finding a way to be there in a way that is meaningful to a neighbor. Get to know their children; invite someone to walk with you; learn the names of the dogs they are walking; volunteer to bring the trash cans in when they leave town; tip the pizza delivery person extra to help them pay for gasoline.

The important thing to remember is that we can either add to the body budgets of people around us, or we can decrease their body budgets. And our body budgets are also similarly influenced by other people. In a sense, we all have the capacity to be Supermen and Superwomen when we go through life wearing invisible positivity capes that help us bring bits of joy into the world, one encounter at a time.

> *Our prime purpose in this life is to help others. And if you can't help them, at least don't hurt them.*
>
> —Dalai Lama

Our small acts of kindness can make a real difference in the lives of others. A wonderful example occurred via my cousins, Sherry, Maribeth, and Susie, in St. Louis. These three sisters brought lunch to my parents every so often during the pandemic, for no particular occasion, just to spread some joy. They provided the table, tablecloth, flowers, plates, and utensils, setting up everything in my mom and dad's driveway. Possessing culinary skills that are somehow missing in my DNA, they created tasty dishes that delighted my parents. Leftovers, of course, were much appreciated. Mom and Dad cherished, above all else, the hours spent chatting and sharing stories. My cousins listened intently to stories they surely heard more than once before. The world's struggles and my parents' assorted aches and pains faded into the background amid shared laughter. I will be eternally grateful for their acts of kindness toward my parents, and forever inspired by their generosity and thoughtfulness.

Try This

Is there someone in your life who could use a lift, who would be very grateful for a kind word or gesture? Maybe just ask the sincere question, "How is your heart today?" And then wait to hear the answer.

> *In the end, only three things matter: how much you loved, how gently you lived, and how gracefully you let go of things not meant for you.*
>
> —Jack Kornfield

Have you encountered the term "pebbling?" This term refers to the polished pebbles that male penguins present to their potential mates. Some researchers believe that this simple gesture demonstrates the male's interest in a female that has captured their attention. In essence, he is trying to convince her that he will be a dutiful partner. Why would a gift of buffed pebbles signify this intention? Laying small, smooth stones at the feet of a female helps her prepare a surface for laying eggs, and that surface will stay above the water line.[214] We encourage closer relationships by engaging in human pebbling, too. When we forward someone a funny video, a favorite poem, or a link to an interesting article, we are seeking to connect, to let them know we are thinking of them. Don't we all enjoy hearing that someone has thought of us enough to share a delightful discovery? Each of us conveys our attention in various ways, including through the loving messages we send to friends and family.

We have seen how our words and actions leave a mark on every person we meet. A kind word or deed can lift someone's spirits, while harsh ones can hurt deeply. What we say and do changes the brains and bodies of those around us, for good or bad, perhaps even altering a life in ways you'll never see. So let's walk through our days carrying this awareness with us, strengthening the bonds that connect and support us.

ACKNOWLEDGMENTS

The greatest gift of life is friendship, and I have received it.

—Hubert H. Humphrey

So many wonderful people have supported and encouraged me in my brief walk on earth. It is with abundant gratefulness that I thank them for their friendship and care. Trying to list all of their names is a risky business, so I ask forgiveness if I've forgotten a few. Here goes:

Heartfelt gratitude to my longtime friends Ann, Mary, Amelia, Betty, Lois, Maureen, Jill, Winkie, Colleen, Dan, Beth, Joy, and to my more recent friends Susy, Judy, Amy, Debbie, Jeff, Marcia, Denny, Mary, and Jose; to my coworkers Laura, Marianne, Kathy, Merrie, Cheryl, Eileen, Helen, and Debbie; and to all of my yoga students. A special thanks to my Cards by Anne customers and friends: Your suggestions, care, and affirmation over these many years have meant more to me than you will ever know. Our conversations have lifted me, taught me, and challenged me; a deep bow of thanks to each one of you.

I am also grateful for the support of my Loyola Press family, including Gary Jansen and Maura Poston, my incredibly talented and wise editors. Thanks as well to Joellyn Cicciarelli, Carrie Fryer, John Christensen, Joe Paprocki, and Julianne Stanz: I so appreciate your faith and trust in me!

Our children Sarah, Elizabeth, and Jackson are sources of endless pride, joy, and inspiration, sharing their gifts with us, fulfilling the advice we gave them long ago to *Do what you love and make the world a better place.* Our grandchildren Morgan, Percy, Milly, Sawyer, Mack, and Charlie provide laughter and fun, and keep me happily hopping, both mentally and physically.

Finally, I wouldn't be writing anything of value without the constant love and support of my one and only love, Jack. He is my encouraging, cheerleading mate who is always ready to listen and honestly respond to my ideas. How I got so lucky, I don't know. But I am deeply and truly grateful that, to quote Fr. John Fonville in our wedding homily on February 20, 1982, we have not "been healed from the gentle wound of true love."

ENDNOTES

Part I Beliefs

1. Alia Crum and Ellen Langer, "Mind-set matters: Exercise and the placebo effect," *Psychological Science* 18, no. 2 (2007): 165–171.

2. Alia Crum et al., "Rethinking stress: The role of mindsets in determining the stress response," *Journal of Personality and Social Psychology* 104, no. 4 (2013): 716–733, https://psycnet.apa.org/doi/10.1037/a0031201.

3. Howard LeWine, ed., "The power of the placebo effect," *Harvard Health Publishing*, July 22, 2024, https://www.health.harvard.edu/newsletter_article/the-power-of-the-placebo-effect.

4. Elissa Patterson and Hans Schroder, "In studies and in real life, placebos have a powerful healing effect on the body and mind," *Michigan Medicine Health Lab*, March 14, 2022, https://www.michiganmedicine.org/health-lab/studies-and-real-life-placebos-have-powerful-healing-effect-body-and-mind.

5. Lysann Damisch et al., "Keep Your Fingers Crossed!: How Superstition Improves Performance," *Psychological Science* 21, no. 7 (2010), https://www.psychologicalscience.org/news/releases/keep-your-fingers-crossed-how-superstition-improves-performance.html.

6. Dacher Keltner, *Awe: The New Science of Everyday Wonder and How It Can Transform Your Life* (Penguin Random House, 2023).

7. Virginia E. Sturm, Samir Datta, Ashlin R. K. Roy, et al., "Big smile, small self: Awe walks promote prosocial positive emotions in older adults," *Emotion* 22, no. 5 (2022): 1044–1058, https://pubmed.ncbi.nlm.nih.gov/32955293/.

8. Maria Monroy and Dacher Keltner, "Awe as a Pathway to Mental and Physical Health," *Perspectives on Psychological Science* 18, no. 2 (2022): 309–320, https://doi.org/10.1177/17456916221094856.

9. Katie Weeman, "Eclipse Psychology: When the Sun and Moon Align, So Do We," *Scientific American*, April 2, 2024, https://www.scientificamerican.com/article/eclipse-psychology-how-the-2024-total-solar-eclipse-will-unite-people/.

10. Summer Allen, "Eight Reasons Why Awe Makes Your Life Better," *Greater Good Magazine*, September 26, 2018, https://greatergood.berkeley.edu/article/item/eight_reasons_why_awe_makes_your_life_better.

11. Barbara Stöckigt et al., "Experiences and Perceived Effects of Rosary Praying: A Qualitative Study," *Journal of Religious Health* 60, no. 6 (2021): 3886–3906, https://pubmed.ncbi.nlm.nih.gov/34106378/.

12. Luciano Bernardi, Peter Sleight, Gabriele Bandinelli, et al., “Effect of rosary prayer and yoga mantras on autonomic cardiovascular rhythms: comparative study,” *British Medical Journal* 323, no. 7327 (2001): 1446–1449, https://pmc.ncbi.nlm.nih.gov/articles/PMC61046/.

13. Logan C. Tice, David E. Eagle, Joshua A. Rash, et al., “The Selah study protocol of three interventions to manage stress among clergy: a preference-based randomized waitlist control trial,” *Trials* 22, no. 892 (2021), https://pubmed.ncbi.nlm.nih.gov/34886896/.

14. Christopher M. Buenrostro and Thomas G. Plante, “A clinical trial of the Examen and mindfulness within a secular substance use disorder treatment program,” *Journal of Addictions & Offender Counseling* 45, no. 1 (2024), https://onlinelibrary.wiley.com/doi/full/10.1002/jaoc.12127.

15. https://cardsbyanne.com/products/dailyexamen.

16. Matt Bradshaw, Christopher G. Ellison, and Jack P. Marcum, “Attachment to God, Images of God, and Psychological Distress in a Nationwide Sample of Presbyterians,” *International Journal for the Psychology of Religion* 20, no. 2 (2010): 130–147, https://doi.org/10.1080/10508611003608049.

17. Barbara L. Fredrickson et al., “Open Hearts Build Lives: Positive Emotions, Induced Through Loving-Kindness Meditation, Build Consequential Personal Resources,” *Journal of Personality and Social Psychology* 95, no. 5 (2008): 1045–1062, https://doi.org/10.1037/a0013262.

18. Melissa A. Rosenkranz, Antoine Lutz, David M. Perlman, et al., “Reduced stress and inflammatory responsiveness in experienced meditators compared to a matched healthy control group,” *Psychoneuroendocrinology* 68 (2016): 117–125, https://doi.org/10.1016/j.psyneuen.2016.02.013.

19. Jennifer S. Mascaro et al., “Compassion meditation enhances empathic accuracy and related neural activity,” *Social Cognitive and Affective Neuroscience* 8, no. 1 (2013): 48–55, https://doi.org/10.1093/scan/nss095.

20. Kristen Rogers, “The psychological benefits of prayer: What science says about the mind-soul connection,” *CNN*, June 17, 2020, https://www.cnn.com/2020/06/17/health/benefits-of-prayer-wellness.

21. Jessie Dezutter et al., “Prayer and pain: the mediating role of positive re-appraisal,” *Journal of Behavioral Medicine* 34, no. 6 (2011): 542–549, https://pubmed.ncbi.nlm.nih.gov/21516338/.

22. Alfia Calderone, et al., "Neurobiological Changes Induced by Mindfulness and Meditation: A Systematic Review," *Biomedicines* 12, no. 11 (2024): 2613, https://doi.org/10.3390/biomedicines12112613.

23. Lisa Miller, Ravi Bansal, Priya Wickframaratne, et al., "Neuroanatomical Correlates of Religiosity and Spirituality: A Study in Adults at High and Low Familial Risk for Depression," *JAMA Psychiatry* 71, no. 12 (2014): 128–135, https://pubmed.ncbi.nlm.nih.gov/24369341/.

24. "Top 10 Health Benefits of Praying," *Health Fitness Revolution*, May 21, 2015, https://www.healthfitnessrevolution.com/top-10-health-benefits-praying.

25. Randy A. Sansone and Lori A. Sansone, "Gratitude and Well Being: The Benefits of Appreciation," *Psychiatry (Edgmont)* 7, no. 11 (2010): 18–22, https://pubmed.ncbi.nlm.nih.gov/21191529/.

26. Brian Levy et al., "Gratitude, affect balance, and stress buffering: A growth curve examination of cardiovascular responses to a laboratory stress task," *International Journal of Psychophysiology* 183 (2023): 103–116, https://www.sciencedirect.com/science/article/abs/pii/S0167876022002707.

27. L. E. Wallace, R. Anthony, C. M. End, and B. M. Way, "Does Religion Stave Off the Grave? Religious Affiliation in One's Obituary and Longevity," *Social Psychological and Personality Science*, 2018, 10(5): 662–670, https://upperroomgathering.com/wp-content/uploads/Documents/Religion/Wallace-Anthony-End-Way-DoesReligionStaveOffTheGrave.pdf.

28. Jean Barcelona et al., "Frontal alpha asymmetry during prayerful and resting states: An EEG study in Catholic Sisters," *International Journal of Psychophysiology* 155 (2020): 9–15, https://doi.org/10.1016/j.ijpsycho.2020.04.019.

29. K. Harinath, A. S. Malhotra, K. Pal, et al., "Effects of Hatha yoga and Omkar meditation on cardiorespiratory performance, psychologic profile, and melatonin secretion," *Journal of Alternative and Complementary Medicine*, April 10, 2004 (2): 261–268, https://pubmed.ncbi.nlm.nih.gov/15165407/.

30. Becca Levy, *Breaking the Age Code: How Your Beliefs About Aging Determine How Long and Well You Live* (William Morrow, 2022).

31. Becca R. Levy et al., "Positive Age Beliefs Protect Against Dementia Even Among Elders with High-Risk Gene," *PLoS One* 13, no. 2 (2018), https://journals.plos.org/plosone/article?id=10.1371/journal.pone.0191004.

32. Jessica Stillman, "A Yale Psychologist Says This Simple Mindset Change Helps People Live 7.5 Years Longer on Average," *Inc.*, August 26, 2024, https://www.inc.com/jessica-stillman/yale-psychologist-simple-mindset-change-helps-people-live-7.5-years-longer-average.html.

33. Becca Levy, "Challenging Age Beliefs in Medicine," virtual interview for Moving Medicine series, American Medical Association, posted July 5, 2022, video, 18:57, https://www.ama-assn.org/delivering-care/population-care/how-positive-age-beliefs-can-support-positive-health-outcomes-becca.

34. Ellen J. Langer, *Counterclockwise: Mindful Health and the Power of Possibility* (Ballantine Books, 2009).

35. Ellen J. Langer, *The Mindful Body: Thinking Our Way to Chronic Health* (Ballantine Books, 2023).

36. Peter Aungle and Ellen Langer, “Physical healing as a function of perceived time,” *Scientific Reports* 13, article no. 22432 (2023), https://www.nature.com/articles/s41598-023-50009-3.

37. Deirdre A. Robertson et al., “Negative Perceptions of Aging and Decline in Walking Speed: A Self-Fulfilling Prophecy,” *PLoS One* 10, no. 4 (2015), https://journals.plos.org/plosone/article?id=10.1371/journal.pone.0123260.

38. Aditi Shrikant, “The No. 1 Personality Trait Linked to Long Life,” *CNBC*, September 17, 2023, https://www.cnbc.com/2023/09/17/this-is-the-nopoint1-personality-trait-linked-to-living-longer.html.

39. Britta K. Hölzel et al., “How Does Mindfulness Meditation Work? Proposing Mechanisms of Action From a Conceptual and Neural Perspective,” *Perspectives on Psychological Science* 6, no. 6 (2011): 537–59, https://pubmed.ncbi.nlm.nih.gov/26168376/.

40. Angeles Arrien, *The Four-Fold Way: Walking the Paths of the Warrior, Teacher, Healer, and Visionary* (HarperSanFrancisco, 1993).

41. Sara Sloat, “The Plight of the Eldest Daughter,” *The Atlantic*, November 14, 2023, https://www.theatlantic.com/family/archive/2023/11/first-born-children-eldest-daughter-family-dynamics/675986/.

42. Debra Fulghum Bruce, “How Worrying Affects the Body,” *WebMD*, November 22, 2024, https://www.webmd.com/balance/how-worrying-affects-your-body.

43. Marc Hrymoc, ed., “The Science Behind Gratitude and Happiness,” *Mental Health Center Cedars Sinai*, November 22, 2024, https://www.mentalhealthctr.com/the-science-behind-gratitude-and-happiness-2/#The_Science_Behind_Gratitude_and_Happiness.

44. Madhuleena Roy Chowdhury, “The Neuroscience of Gratitude and Effects on the Brain,” *Positive Psychology*, April 9, 2019, https://positivepsychology.com/neuroscience-of-gratitude/.

Part II Bodies

45. Luciano Bernardi et al., “Effect of rosary prayer and yoga mantras on autonomic cardiovascular rhythms: comparative study,” *British Medical Journal* 323, no. 7327 (2001): 1446–1449, https://doi.org/10.1136/bmj.323.7327.1446.

46. Chittaranjan Andrade and Rajiv Radhakrishnan, “Prayer and healing: A medical and scientific perspective on randomized controlled trials,” *Indian Journal of Psychiatry* 51, no. 4 (2009): 247–253, https://doi.org/10.4103/0019-5545.58288.

47. Ravinder Jerath et al., “Self-regulation of breathing as a primary treatment for anxiety,” *Applied Psychophysiology and Biofeedback* 40, no. 2 (2015): 105–117, https://doi.org/10.1007/s10484-015-9279-8.

48. H. J. Schünemann et al., "Pulmonary function is a long-term predictor of mortality in the general population: 29-year follow-up of the Buffalo Health Study," *Chest* 118, no. 3, (2000): 656–664, https://pubmed.ncbi.nlm.nih.gov/10988186/.

49. Tanya G. K. Bentley, Gina D'Andrea-Penna, Marina Rakic, et al., "Breathing Practices for Stress and Anxiety Reduction: Conceptual Framework of Implementation Guidelines Based on a Systematic Review of the Published Literature," *Brain Sciences* 13, no. 12 (2023): 1612, https://www.mdpi.com/2076-3425/13/12/1612.

50. Melis Yilmaz Balban et al., "Brief structured respiration practices enhance mood and reduce physiological arousal," *Cell Reports Medicine* 4, no. 1 (2023), https://doi.org/10.1016/j.xcrm.2022.100895.

51. B. Grace Bullock, "How Your Breath Controls Your Mood and Attention," *Mindful*, September 5, 2019, https://www.mindful.org/how-your-breath-controls-your-mood-and-attention/.

52. James Nestor, *Breath: The New Science of a Lost Art* (Riverhead Books, 2020), 19–33.

53. Masahiro Sano et al., "Increased oxygen load in the prefrontal cortex from mouth breathing: a vector-based near-infrared spectroscopy study," *NeuroReport* 24, no. 17 (2013): 934–940, https://doi.org/10.1097/WNR.0000000000000008.

54. James Nestor, *Breath: The New Science of a Lost Art*, 19–33.

55. Maria Elide Vanutelli et al., "Breathing Right...or Left! The Effects of Unilateral Nostril Breathing on Psychological and Cognitive Wellbeing: A Pilot Study," *Brain Sciences* 14, no. 4 (2024): 302, https://doi.org/10.3390/brainsci14040302.

56. F. Zeidan, "Mindfulness meditation-related pain relief: Evidence for unique brain mechanisms in the regulation of pain," *Neuroscience Letters* 520, no. 2 (2012): 165–173, https://doi.org/10.1016/j.neulet.2012.03.082.

57. R. Zoffness and M. A. Schumacher, *The Pain Management Workbook: Powerful CBT and Mindfulness Skills to Take Control of Pain and Reclaim Your Life* (New Harbinger Publications, 2020).

58. The Pain Psychology Center, https://painpsychologycenter.com.

59. Andrew Huberman, "Using Light for Health," *Huberman Lab Neural Network Newsletter*, January 24, 2023, https://www.hubermanlab.com/newsletter/using-light-for-health.

60. Jessica Del Pozo, "Sleep: The Power of Dusk and Dawn," *Psychology Today*, July 31, 2023, https://www.psychologytoday.com/us/blog/being-awake-better/202307/sleep-the-power-of-dusk-and-dawn.

61. Lisa Marshall, "Get Morning Light, Sleep Better at Night," *WebMD*, March 23, 2022, https://www.webmd.com/sleep-disorders/features/morning-light-better-sleep.

62. Peter Aspinall et al., "The urban brain: analysing outdoor physical activity with mobile EEG," *British Journal of Sports Medicine* 49, no. 4 (2015): 272–276, https://doi.org/10.1136/bjsports-2012-091877.

63. Sarah Hanson and Andy Jones, "Is there evidence that walking groups have health benefits?," *British Journal of Sports Medicine* 49, no. 11 (2015): 710–715, https://bjsm.bmj.com/content/49/11/710.

64. Mandy Erickson, "Setting your biological clock, reducing stress while sheltering in place," *Stanford Medicine*, June 3, 2020, https://med.stanford.edu/news/insights/2020/06/setting-your-biological-clock-reducing-stress-while-sheltering-in-place.html.

65. Precision Eye Care, "The Role of Dopamine in Myopia," August 30, 2023, https://precisioneyemd.com/2023/08/30/dopamine-in-myopia/.

66. Gareth Lingham, Seyhan Yazar, Robyn M. Lucas, et al., "Time spent outdoors in childhood is associated with reduced risk of myopia as an adult," *Scientific Reports* 11, 6337 (2023), https://doi.org/10.1038/s41598-021-85825-y.

67. Manoush Zomorodi et al., "The story behind soaring myopia among kids," *NPR*, October 17, 2023, https://www.npr.org/2023/10/17/1200611635/the-story-behind-soaring-myopia-among-children.

68. Casey Eye Institute, "Myopia on the rise, especially among children," June 3, 2022, https://www.ohsu.edu/casey-eye-institute/myopia-rise-especially-among-children.

69. Carlo Maria Di Liegro, "Physical Activity and Brain Health," *Genes (Basel)* 10, no. 9 (2019): 720, https://doi.org/10.3390/genes10090720.

70. Telomeres are the endcaps of our chromosomes that protect our cells from damage and degradation, analogous to the plastic ends of shoelaces. They protect our DNA from damage and from fraying prematurely. Telomerase is the enzyme that keeps telomeres functioning well. When people exercised at least three times per week, their telomerase levels doubled after just six months. Aerobic exercise produces the greatest increase in telomerase, and the more categories of exercise people engage in, the longer their telomeres.

71. Halil İbrahim Ceylan, Mehmet Ertuğrul Öztürk, Deniz Öztürk, et al., "Acute effect of moderate and high-intensity interval exercises on asprosin and BDNF levels in inactive normal weight and obese individuals," *Scientific Reports* 13, 7040 (2023), https://www.nature.com/articles/s41598-023-34278-6.

72. Mayoorey Murugathasan, Ardavan Jafari, Amandeep Amandeep, et al., "Moderate exercise induces trained immunity in macrophages," *American Journal of Physiology-Cell Psychology* 325, no. 2 (2023), https://journals.physiology.org/doi/full/10.1152/ajpcell.00130.2023.

73. Arash Javanbakht, "How Exercise Keeps Your Brain Healthy and Protects It Against Depression and Anxiety," *Neuroscience News*, February 26, 2021, https://neurosciencenews.com/exercise-brain-mental-health-17903.

74. Angelika Schmitt, Neeraj Upadhyay, Jason Anthony Martin, et al., "Modulation of Distinct Intrinsic Resting State Brain Networks by Acute Exercise Bouts of Differing Intensity," *Brain Plasticity* 5, no. 1 (2019): 33–55, https://pubmed.ncbi.nlm.nih.gov/31970059/.

75. Harvard Health Publishing, "Harder workout intensity may not increase your longevity," *Harvard Health Publishing*, January 1, 2021, https://www.health.harvard.edu/staying-healthy/harder-workout-intensity-may-not-increase-your-longevity.

76. Angela Haupt, "Backward Walking Is the Best Workout You're Not Doing," *TIME*, May 7, 2024, https://time.com/6975058/backward-walking-health-benefits/.

77. Daniel Preiato, "Is Walking After Eating Good for You?," *Healthline*, August 12, 2024, https://www.healthline.com/nutrition/walking-after-eating.

78. Pekka Oja, Paul Kelly, Zeljko Pedisic, et al., "Associations of specific types of sports and exercise with all-cause and cardiovascular-disease mortality: A cohort study of 80,306 British adults," *British Journal of Sports Medicine* 51, no. 10 (2017): 812–817, https://doi.org/10.1136/bjsports-2016-096822.

79. Centers for Disease Control and Prevention, "Adult Activity: An Overview," December 20, 2023, https://www.cdc.gov/physical-activity-basics/guidelines/adults.html.

80. Melinda Hahm, "Isometric exercise: Using body weight to lower blood pressure," *Mayo Clinic Health System*, January 22, 2024, https://www.mayoclinichealthsystem.org/hometown-health/speaking-of-health/isometric-exercise-and-blood-pressure.

81. Austin Perlmutter, "The Surprising Brain-Health Benefits of Weightlifting," *Psychology Today*, February 14, 2024, https://www.psychologytoday.com/us/blog/the-modern-brain/202402/the-surprising-benefits-of-weightlifting-for-brain-health.

82. Jari A. Laukkanen et al, "Cardiovascular and Other Health Benefits of Sauna Bathing: A Review of the Evidence," *Mayo Clinic Proceedings* 93, no. 8 (2018), 1111–1121, https://doi.org/10.1016/j.mayocp.2018.04.008.

83. Corrie Pelc, "Heat therapy may lead to better outcomes in treating depression than cold exposure," *Medical News Today*, February 9, 2024, https://www.medicalnewstoday.com/articles/heat-therapy-sauna-better-outcomes-treating-depression-cold-exposure.

84. Chinta Sidharthan, "The Science of Sauna & Heat Exposure," *News Medical*, April 9, 2025, https://www.news-medical.net/health/What-Saunas-Really-Do-to-Your-Brain-and-Body.aspx.; Tanjaniina Laukkanen et al., "Sauna bathing is inversely associated with dementia and Alzheimer's disease in middle-aged Finnish men," *Age and Ageing* 46, no. 2 (2017): 245–249, https://pubmed.ncbi.nlm.nih.gov/27932366/.

85. Tanjaniina Laukkanen et al., "Association between sauna bathing and fatal cardiovascular and all-cause mortality events," *JAMA Internal Medicine* 175, no. 4 (2015): 542–548, https://doi.org/10.1001/jamainternmed.2014.8187.

86. Johns Hopkins Medicine, "9 Benefits of Yoga," https://www.hopkinsmedicine.org/health/wellness-and-prevention/9-benefits-of-yoga.

87. Stephanie Voss et al., "Yoga Impacts Cognitive Health: Neurophysiological Changes and Stress Regulation Mechanisms," *Exercise and Sport Sciences Reviews* 51, no. 2 (2022): 73–81, https://doi.org/10.1249/JES.0000000000000311.

88. Yi-Hsueh Lu et al., "Twelve-Minute Daily Yoga Regimen Reverses Osteoporotic Bone Loss," *Topics in Geriatric Rehabilitation* 31, no. 2 (2015): 81–87, https://pubmed.ncbi.nlm.nih.gov/27226695/.

89. Corjena Cheung et al., "Yoga for managing knee osteoarthritis in older women: a pilot randomized controlled trial," *BMC Complementary and Alternative Medicine* 14, no. 160 (2014), https://doi.org/10.1186/1472-6882-14-160.

90. Andrew Gregory, "Ultra-processed food linked to 32 harmful effects to health, review finds," *The Guardian*, February 28, 2024, https://www.theguardian.com/society/2024/feb/28/ultra-processed-food-32-harmful-effects-health-review.

91. Christopher M. Palmer, *Brain Energy: A Revolutionary Breakthrough in Understanding Mental Health—and Improving Treatment for Anxiety, Depression, OCD, PTSD, and More* (BenBella Books, 2022).

92. Zheyi Song et al., "Effects of ultra-processed foods on the microbiota-gut-brain axis: The bread-and-butter issue," *Food Research International* 167 (2023), https://doi.org/10.1016/j.foodres.2023.112730.

93. Tony Hicks, "Ultra-processed foods may be as addictive as smoking, study says," *Medical News Today*, October 18, 2023, https://www.medicalnewstoday.com/articles/ultra-processed-foods-may-be-as-addictive-as-smoking-study-says.

94. Sarah Garone, "What's the Difference Between Processed and Ultra-Processed Food?," *Healthline*, May 8, 2023, https://www.healthline.com/health/food-nutrition/ultra-processed-foods.

95. Anna M.R. Hayes, Logan Tierno Lauer, Alicia E. Kao, et al., "Western diet consumption impairs memory function via dysregulated hippocampus acetylcholine signaling," *Brain, Behavior, and Immunity* 118 (2024): 408–422, https://doi.org/10.1016/j.bbi.2024.03.015.

96. Stony Brook University, "Low-Carb Diet Could Boost Brain Health, Study Finds," September 4, 2020, https://news.stonybrook.edu/featuredpost/low-carb-diet-could-boost-brain-health-study-finds/.

97. Preethi Srikanthan and Arun S. Karlamangla, "Muscle Mass Index as a Predictor of Longevity in Older Adults," *The American Journal of Medicine* 127, no. 6 (2014): 547–553, https://doi.org/10.1016/j.amjmed.2014.02.007.

98. Howard LeWine, ed., "Foods linked to better brainpower," *Harvard Health Publishing*, April 3, 2024, https://www.health.harvard.edu/healthbeat/foods-linked-to-better-brainpower.

99. Allison Torres Burtka, "What Are REM Sleep and Non-REM Sleep?" *WebMD*, July 11, 2024, https://www.webmd.com/sleep-disorders/sleep-101.

100. Matthew Walker, *Why We Sleep* (Penguin Books, 2018).

101. Corrie Pelc, "Reducing night light exposure may be a simple way to cut diabetes risk," *Medical News Today*, September 4, 2024, https://www.medicalnewstoday.com/articles/reducing-night-light-exposure-simple-way-cut-diabetes-risk.

102. Vijay Kumar Malesu, "Study finds link between nighttime light exposure and increased Alzheimer's disease risk," *News Medical*, September 10, 2024, https://www.news-medical.net/news/20240910/Study-finds-link-between-nighttime-light-exposure-and-increased-Alzheimers-disease-risk.aspx.

103. Elisa M.S. Meth, Luiz Eduardo Mateus Brandão, Lieve T. van Egmond, et al., "A weighted blanket increases pre-sleep salivary concentrations of melatonin in young, healthy adults," *Journal of Sleep Research* 32, no. 2 (2023), https://onlinelibrary.wiley.com/doi/10.1111/jsr.13743.

104. Corrie Pelc, "How the brain flushes out toxic proteins that may lead to cognitive decline," *Medical News Today*, October 14, 2024, https://www.medicalnewstoday.com/articles/how-the-brain-flushes-out-toxic-proteins-that-may-lead-to-cognitive-decline.

105. David Wright, "On your back? Side? Face-down? Mice show how we sleep may trigger or protect our brain from diseases like ALS," *The Conversation*, May 26, 2022, https://theconversation.com/on-your-back-side-face-down-mice-show-how-we-sleep-may-trigger-or-protect-our-brain-from-diseases-like-als-181954.

106. See https://insighttimer.com or https://www.calm.com.

107. Zachary Zamore and Sigrid C. Veasy, "Neural consequences of chronic sleep disruption," *Trends in Neurosciences* 45, no. 9 (2022): 678–691, https://pubmed.ncbi.nlm.nih.gov/35691776/.

108. Jorge F.T. de Souza et al., "High-Intensity Interval Training Attenuates Insulin Resistance Induced by Sleep Deprivation in Healthy Males," *Frontiers in Physiology* 8 (2017): 992, https://doi.org/10.3389/fphys.2017.00992.

109. Daniel P. Windred, Angus C. Burns, Jacqueline M. Lane, et al., "Sleep regularity is a stronger predictor of mortality risk than sleep duration: A prospective cohort study," *Sleep* 47, no. 1 (2024), https://academic.oup.com/sleep/article/47/1/zsad253/7280269.

110. Kevin Jiang, "Sleep, death, and…the gut?" *The Harvard Gazette*, June 4, 2020, https://news.harvard.edu/gazette/story/2020/06/study-reveals-guts-role-in-causing-death-by-sleep-deprivation/.

111. Tina Sundelin et al., "Negative effects of restricted sleep on facial appearance and social appeal," *Royal Society Open Science* 4, no. 5 (2017), https://royalsocietypublishing.org/doi/10.1098/rsos.160918.

112. Maria Popova, "A Responsibility to Wonder: Pioneering Neuroscientist Charles Scott Sherrington on the Spirituality of Nature," *The Marginalian*, October 16, 2022, https://www.themarginalian.org/2022/09/19/beryl-markham-west-with-the-night/.

113. Matthew 6:26 (NRSV).

114. Qing Li, "Effect of forest bathing trips on human immune function," *Environmental Health and Preventive Medicine* 15, no. 1 (2009): 9–17, https://doi.org/10.1007/s12199-008-0068-3.

115. Molly McDonough, "A Walk in the Woods May Boost Mental Health," *Harvard Medicine*, Summer 2023, https://magazine.hms.harvard.edu/articles/walk-woods-may-boost-mental-health.

116. Cassie Holmes, *Happier Hour: How to Beat Distraction, Expand Your Time, and Focus on What Matters Most* (Gallery Books, 2022).

117. Eric Ralls, "Being in nature changes our overall perception of time," *Earth.com*, March 6, 2024, https://www.earth.com/news/nature-experiences-alter-time-perception/.

118. King's College London, "Feeling chirpy: Being around birds is linked to lasting mental health benefits," October 27, 2022, https://www.kcl.ac.uk/news/feeling-chirpy-being-around-birds-is-linked-to-lasting-mental-health-benefits.

119. E. Stobbe et al., "Birdsongs alleviate anxiety and paranoia in healthy participants," *Scientific Reports* 12, 16414 (2022), https://www.nature.com/articles/s41598-022-20841-0.

120. Will Hall, "9 Life Lessons from Birds," *Birda*, March 31, 2023, https://birda.org/life-lessons-from-birds/.

121. George F. Young, Luca Scardovi, Andrea Cavagna, Irene Giardina, Naomi E. Leonard, "Starling Flock Networks Manage Uncertainty in Consensus at Low Cost," *PLoS Comput Biol*, 9(1): e1002894 (2013), https://journals.plos.org/ploscompbiol/article?id=10.1371/journal.pcbi.1002894.

Part III Brains

122. Matthew A. Killingsworth and Daniel T. Gilbert, "A Wandering Mind is an Unhappy Mind," *Science* 330, no. 6006 (2010): 932, https://www.science.org/doi/10.1126/science.1192439.

123. Johann Hari, *Stolen Focus: Why You Can't Pay Attention—and How to Think Deeply Again* (Crown Publishing Group, 2022).

124. Adam Gazzaley and Larry D. Rosen, *The Distracted Mind: Ancient Brains in a High-Tech World* (MIT Press, 2016).

125. Harvard Health Publishing, "4 ways to improve focus and memory," February 7, 2025, https://www.health.harvard.edu/mind-and-mood/4-ways-to-improve-focus-and-memory.

126. American Psychological Association, "Multitasking: Switching costs," March 20, 2006, https://www.apa.org/topics/research/multitasking.

127. Amir Baniassadi et al., "Home Ambient Temperature and Self-Reported Attention in Community-Dwelling Older Adults," *The Journals of Gerontology: Series A* 80, no. 4 (2025), https://doi.org/10.1093/gerona/glae286.

128. James Clear, "3-2-1 Newsletter," March 21, 2024, https://jamesclear.com/3-2-1/march-21-2024.

129. Elisabeth Almekinder, "Niksen: The Duth Art of Purposefully Doing Nothing," *BlueZones*, https://www.bluezones.com/2019/11/niksen-the-dutch-art-of-purposefully-doing-nothing/.

130. Greg Miller, "Peering Inside the Wandering Mind," *Science*, January 18, 2007, https://www.science.org/content/article/peering-inside-wandering-mind.

131. Shona Gosh, "A former Google strategist says tech is warping our attention spans—and it's terrible for humanity," *Business Insider*, May 31, 2018, https://www.businessinsider.com/google-philosopher-james-williams-tech-distraction-bad-humanity-2018-5.

132. Amishi P. Jha, *Peak Mind: Find Your Focus, Own Your Attention, Invest 12 Minutes a Day* (HarperOne, 2021).

133. Ethan Kross, *Chatter: The Voice in Our Head, Why It Matters, and How to Harness It* (Crown, 2021).

134. Shirley Leanos, Esra Kürüm, Carla M. Strickland-Hughes, et al., "The Impact of Learning Multiple Real-World Skills on Cognitive Abilities and Functional Independence in Healthy Older Adults," *The Journals of Gerontology: Series B* 78, no. 8, (2023): 1305–1317, https://doi.org/10.1093/geronb/gbad053.

135. Paul Ian Cross, "White matter in superagers' brains is less prone to aging and cognitive decline," *Medical News Today*, May 14, 2024, https://www.medicalnewstoday.com/articles/white-matter-in-superagers-brains-is-less-prone-to-aging-and-cognitive-decline.

136. Jessica Stillman, "Neuroscience Says Doing This for Just 1 Hour a Week Can Make Your Brain 5 Years Younger," *Inc*, July 15, 2024, https://www.inc.com/jessica-stillman/neuroscience-do-this-1-hour-week-make-brain-5-years-younger.html.

137. The Society for Personality and Social Psychology, "New study shows meaningful social interactions boost well-being, but context matters," *Phys.org*, June 28, 2024, https://phys.org/news/2024-06-meaningful-social-interactions-boost-context.html.

138. Rachel Wu and Jessica A. Church-Lang, "To Stay Sharp as You Age, Learn New Skills," *Scientific American*, June 29, 2023, https://www.scientificamerican.com/article/to-stay-sharp-as-you-age-learn-new-skills/.

139. Jill Suttie, "Five Ways to Keep Your Brain Healthy as You Age," *Greater Good Magazine*, May 11, 2021, https://greatergood.berkeley.edu/article/item/five_ways_to_keep_your_brain_healthy_as_you_age.

140. Fiona Sally Miller, "Exercise has the same effect on the brain as coffee," *Medical News Today*, January 30, 2020, https://www.medicalnewstoday.com/articles/exercise-boosts-memory-like-caffeine.

141. Anisa Morava et al., "Effects of Caffeine and Acute Aerobic Exercise on Working Memory and Caffeine Withdrawal," *Scientific Reports* 9, 19644 (2019), https://doi.org/10.1038/s41598-019-56251-y.

142. Y. Takayanagi et al., "Accuracy of Reports of Lifetime Mental and Physical Disorders: Results From the Baltimore Epidemiological Catchment Area Study," *JAMA Psychiatry* 71, no. 3 (2014): 273–280.

143. National Institute of Mental Health, "Major Depression," Accessed April 16, 2025, https://www.nimh.nih.gov/health/statistics/major-depression.

144. Lowri Dowthwaite-Walsh, "The Paradox of Progress: Why More Freedom Isn't Making Women Happier," *Neuroscience News*, September 3, 2023, https://neurosciencenews.com/women-happiness-psychology-23862/.

145. Zawn Villines, "Effects of gender discrimination on health," *Medical News Today*, June 23, 2021, https://www.medicalnewstoday.com/articles/effects-of-gender-discrimination.

146. Norman Farb and Zindel Segal, "Paying Attention to Sensations Can Help Reset the Mind," *Scientific American*, March 8, 2024, https://www.scientificamerican.com/article/paying-attention-to-sensations-can-help-reset-the-mind/.

147. Angela Thoreson, "Helping people, changing lives: 3 health benefits of volunteering," *Mayo Clinic Health System*, August 1, 2003, https://www.mayoclinichealthsystem.org/hometown-health/speaking-of-health/3-health-benefits-of-volunteering.

148. Alexandra Touroutoglou et al., "The Tenacious Brain: How the Anterior Mid-Cingulate Contributes to Achieving Goals," *Cortex* 123 (2019): 12–29, https://pmc.ncbi.nlm.nih.gov/articles/PMC7381101/.

149. Center for Substance Abuse Treatment (US), "Understanding the Impact of Trauma," in *Treatment Improvement Protocol (TIP) Series, No. 57, Trauma-Informed Care in Behavioral Health Services* (Abuse and Mental Health Services Administration, 2014), https://www.ncbi.nlm.nih.gov/books/NBK207191/.

150. Brechen MacRae, "Thich Nhat Hanh Walking Meditation," *The Mindful Stoic*, July 21, 2020, https://mindfulstoic.net/mindful-walking/.

151. James Clear, "3-2-1 Newsletter," June 11, 2020, https://jamesclear.com/3-2-1/june-11-2020.

152. Etty Hillesum, *An Interrupted Life: The Diaries, 1941–1943 and Letters from Westerbork*, trans. Arnold J. Pomerans (Henry Holt and Company, 1996).

153. Paul E. Jose, Bee T. Lim, and Fred B. Bryant, "Does Savoring Increase Happiness? A Daily Diary Study," *The Journal of Positive Psychology* 7, no. 3 (2012): 176–187, https://doi.org/10.1080/17439760.2012.671345.

154. Jessica Stillman, "Neuroscience Says This Brainless Activity Reduces Stress and Quiets Your Mind (but Only If You Do It This Specific Way)," *Inc.*, January 29, 2024, https://www.inc.com/jessica-stillman/neuroscience-says-brainless-activity-reduces-stress-quiets-mind-specific-way.html.

155. Denis Storey, "Handwriting Shows Unexpected Benefits Over Typing," *Psychiatrist.com*, January 30, 2024, https://www.psychiatrist.com/news/handwriting-shows-unexpected-benefits-over-typing/.

156. Denis Storey, "Gut Microbiome Breakthroughs Revolutionize Schizophrenia Treatment," *Psychiatrist.com*, January 15, 2025, https://www.psychiatrist.com/news/gut-microbiome-breakthroughs-revolutionize-schizophrenia-treatment/.

157. Andrew Huberman, host, *The Huberman Lab*, podcast, "How to Build, Maintain & Repair Gut Health with Dr. Justin Sonnenburg," March 7, 2022, https://www.youtube.com/watch?v=ouCWNRvPk20.

158. *Speaking of Psychology*, podcast, episode 78, "The mind-gut connection, with Faith Dickerson, PhD, and Emeran Mayer, MD," 2019, https://www.apa.org/news/podcasts/speaking-of-psychology/mind-gut-connection.

159. Jill Suttie, "Four Funny Ways Laughter Is Good for You," *Greater Good Magazine*, June 27, 2023, https://greatergood.berkeley.edu/article/item/four_funny_ways_laughter_is_good_for_you.

160. L. E. Kurtz and S. B. Algoe, "Putting Laughter in Context: Shared Laughter as Behavioral Indicator of Relationship Well-Being," *Personal Relationships*, Dec 1, 2015, 22(4): 573–590, https://pubmed.ncbi.nlm.nih.gov/26957946/.

161. Don Colburn, "Norman Cousins, Still Laughing," *The Washington Post*, October 20, 1986, https://www.washingtonpost.com/archive/lifestyle/wellness/1986/10/21/norman-cousins-still-laughing/e17f23cb-3e8c-4f58-b907-2dcd00326e22/.

162. R.I.M. Dunbar, R. Baron, A. Frangou, et al., "Social Laughter Is Correlated with an Elevated Pain Threshold," *Proceedings of the Royal Society B: Biological Sciences* 279, no. 1731 (2012): 1161–1167, https://doi.org/10.1098/rspb.2011.1373.

163. Janet M. Gibson, "Laughing Is Good for Your Mind and Your Body, Here's What the Research Shows," *Neuroscience News*, November 29, 2020, https://neurosciencenews.com/laughter-physical-mental-psychology-17339/.

164. JongEun Yim, "Therapeutic Benefits of Laughter in Mental Health: A Theoretical Review," *The Tohoku Journal of Experimental Medicine* 239, no. 3 (2016): 243–249, https://doi.org/10.1620/tjem.239.243.

165. Aytug Altundag, Melih Cayonu, Gurkan Kayabasoglu, et al., "Modified olfactory training in patients with postinfectious olfactory loss," *Laryngoscope* 125, no. 8 (2015): 1763–1766, https://pubmed.ncbi.nlm.nih.gov/26031472/.

166. Justin Cottrell, Josie Xu, Michael Au, Eric Monteiro, Ian Witterick, and Allan Vescan, "Smell Training," https://www.neilmed.com/articles/smell-restore/Smell%20Training%20Sinai%20Handout.pdf.

167. Cynthia C. Woo, Blake Miranda, Mithra Sathishkumar, et al., "Overnight olfactory enrichment using an odorant diffuser improves memory and modifies the uncinate fasciculus in older adults," *Frontiers in Neuroscience* 14 (2023), https://doi.org/10.3389/fnins.2023.1200448.

168. Denise Mann, "12 Diseases Doctors Can Actually Detect Through Smell," *The Healthy*, February 1, 2021, https://www.thehealthy.com/ear-nose-throat/diseases-doctors-can-smell/.

Part IV Bonds

169. Julianne Holt-Lunstad, Timothy B. Smith, and J. Bradley Layton, "Social relationships and mortality risk: a meta-analytic review," *PLoS Medicine* 7, no. 7 (2010), https://doi.org/10.1371/journal.pmed.1000316.

170. US Department of Health and Human Services, *Our Epidemic of Loneliness and Isolation: The U.S. Surgeon General's Advisory on the Healing Effects of Social Connection and Community* (Department of Health and Human Services, 2023), https://www.hhs.gov/sites/default/files/surgeon-general-social-connection-advisory.pdf.

171. American Heart Association, "Social isolation and loneliness increase the risk of death from heart attack, stroke," August 4, 2022, https://newsroom.heart.org/news/social-isolation-and-loneliness-increase-the-risk-of-death-from-heart-attack-stroke.

172. John T. Cacioppo and William Patrick, *Loneliness: Human Nature and the Need for Social Connection* (W. W. Norton & Company, 2008).

173. Michele M. Kroll, "Prolonged Social Isolation and Loneliness are Equivalent to Smoking 15 Cigarettes A Day," University of New Hampshire Extension, May 2, 2022, https://extension.unh.edu/blog/2022/05/prolonged-social-isolation-loneliness-are-equivalent-smoking-15-cigarettes-day.

174. Kat Carlton, "What is Loneliness?," *The Forefront, University of Chicago Medicine*, February 14, 2019, https://www.uchicagomedicine.org/forefront/health-and-wellness-articles/what-is-loneliness.

175. Pauline Pérez, Jens Madsen, Leah Banellis, et al., "Conscious processing of narrative stimuli synchronizes heart rate between individuals," *Cell Reports* 36, no. 11 (2021), https://doi.org/10.1016/j.celrep.2021.109692.

176. Marwa Azab, "Is Social Pain Real Pain?," *Psychology Today*, April 25, 2017, https://www.psychologytoday.com/us/blog/neuroscience-in-everyday-life/201704/is-social-pain-real-pain.

177. Micaela De Weck et al., "Hearing Someone Laugh and Seeing Someone Yawn: Modality-Specific Contagion of Laughter and Yawning in the Absence of Others," *Frontiers in Psychology* 13 (2022), https://doi.org/10.3389/fpsyg.2022.780665.

178. T. L. Chartrand and J. A. Bargh, "The chameleon effect: the perception-behavior link and social interaction," *Journal of Personality and Social Psychology* 76, no. 6 (1999): 893–910, https://doi.org/10.1037//0022-3514.76.6.893.

179. University of Colorado at Boulder, "When Lovers Touch, Their Breathing and Heartbeat Syncs While Pain Wanes," *Neuroscience News*, June 21, 2017, https://neurosciencenews.com/empathy-neurobiology-lovers-6951/.

180. Robert J. Waldinger and Marc Schulz, *The Good Life: Lessons from the World's Longest Scientific Study of Happiness* (Simon & Schuster, 2023), 175.

181. University of California—Davis, "New study finds partner's happiness linked to lower stress hormone levels in older couples," *ScienceDaily*, October 22, 2024, http://www.sciencedaily.com/releases/2024/10/241022153820.htm.

182. Michael W. Kraus, Cassey Huang, and Dacher Keltner, "Tactile communication, cooperation, and performance: an ethological study of the NBA", *Emotion* 10, no. 5 (2010): 745–749, https://doi.org/10.1037/a0019382.

183. Michael W. Kraus, Cassey Huang, Dacher Keltner, "Tactile communication, cooperation, and performance: an ethological study of the NBA," *Emotion* 10, no. 5 (2010): 745–749, https://pubmed.ncbi.nlm.nih.gov/21038960/.

184. Paula Span, "They May Be Just Acquaintances. They're Important to You Anyway," *The New York Times*, April 22, 2023, https://www.nytimes.com/2023/04/22/health/seniors-acquaintances-happiness.html.

185. Span, "They May Be Just Acquaintances."

186. Catherine Douglas Moran, "Aisles Abroad: Dutch grocer Jumbo embraces a slower checkout option," *Grocery Dive*, March 28, 2023, https://www.grocerydive.com/news/aisles-abroad-dutch-grocer-jumbo-slow-chat-checkouts/645702/.

187. Malcolm Brabant, "How 'chatty benches' are building connections and combating loneliness in Britain," *PBS News Hour*, December 25, 2023, https://www.pbs.org/newshour/show/how-chatty-benches-are-building-connections-and-combating-loneliness-in-britain.

188. Alexis L. Thomson and Jason T. Siegel, "Elevation: A Review of Scholarship on a Moral and Other-Praising Emotion," *The Journal of Positive Psychology* 12, no. 6 (2017): 628–638, https://www.tandfonline.com/doi/full/10.1080/17439760.2016.1269184.

189. John F. Helliwell, Richard Layard, Jeffrey D. Sachs, et al., eds., *World Happiness Report 2022* (Sustainable Development Solutions Network, 2022).

190. Hillesum, *An Interrupted Life*, 164.

191. Dimitris Xygalatas, *Ritual: How Seemingly Senseless Acts Make Life Worth Living* (Little, Brown Spark, 2022), 219, 227.

192. Frank Waters, *Book of the Hopi* (Viking Press, 1963).

193. Alix Dunham, "The Neuroscience of Ritual," *Be Ceremonial* (blog), April 30, 2024, https://www.beceremonial.com/blog/the-neuroscience-of-ritual/.

194. Dunham, "The Neuroscience of Ritual."

195. Xygalatas, *Ritual*, 103.

196. Paul J. Zak, "Why Weddings Make Us Feel Good," *Psychology Today*, April 18, 2014, https://www.psychologytoday.com/us/blog/the-moral-molecule/201404/why-weddings-make-us-feel-good.

197. Cristine H Legare and André L Souza, "Evaluating ritual efficacy: evidence from the supernatural," *Cognition* 124, no. 1 (2012): 1–15, https://www.sciencedirect.com/science/article/abs/pii/S0010027712000546.

198. Jacqueline Woolley, "The All-Important Annual Birthday Party," *Psychology Today*, January 10, 2013, https://www.psychologytoday.com/us/blog/what-children-know/201301/the-all-important-annual-birthday-party.

199. Kelly McGonigal, *The Joy of Movement: How Exercise Helps Us Find Happiness, Hope, Connection, and Courage* (Avery, 2019).

200. Jacques Launay and Eiluned Pearce, "The New Science of Singing Together," *Greater Good Magazine*, December 4, 2015, https://greatergood.berkeley.edu/article/item/science_of_singing.

201. University of Oxford. "Singing's Secret Power: The Ice-breaker Effect." *University of Oxford News*, October 28, 2015, https://www.ox.ac.uk/news/2015-10-28-singing's-secret-power-ice-breaker-effect-1.

202. Tuomas Koivula, "Music's Universal Impact on Body and Emotion," *Neuroscience News*, January 30, 2024, https://neurosciencenews.com/music-emotion-body-25543/.

203. Neil Theise, "Notes on Complexity: A Scientific Theory of Connection, Consciousness, and Being," *Next Big Idea Club*, https://nextbigideaclub.com/magazine/notes-complexity-scientific-theory-connection-consciousness-bookbite/42793/?srsltid=AfmBOoruuxSZKAqrS3UbAwv6CfZyrKjT9nhDNwYlN62baY7MxeHuIQW-.

204. Melissa Simone, Christian Geiser, and Ginger Lockhart, "The Importance of Face-to-Face Contact and Reciprocal Relationships and their Associations with Depressive Symptoms and Life Satisfaction," *Quality of Life Research* 28, no. 11 (2019): 2909–2917, https://doi.org/10.1007/s11136-019-02232-7.

205. Jill Suttie, "Do You Underestimate the Impact of Being Kind?," *Neuroscience News*, November 21, 2022, https://neurosciencenews.com/kindness-underestimated-21911/.

206. Houston Kraft, *Deep Kindness: A Revolutionary Guide for the Way We Think, Talk, and Act in Kindness* (Simon & Schuster, 2020), 28.

207. Kaeli Swift, Corvid Research, https://corvidresearch.blog/.

208. 1 Cor. 12:25–26 (NRSV).

209. Lisa Feldman Barrett, *Seven and a Half Lessons About the Brain* (Houghton Mifflin Harcourt, 2020), 89.

210. Barrett, *Seven and a Half Lessons About the Brain*, 90.

211. Waldinger and Schulz, *The Good Life*, 10.

212. Barrett, *Seven and a Half Lessons About the Brain*, 93.

213. Barrett, *Seven and a Half Lessons About the Brain*, 95.

214. Selwo Marina, "Why Penguins Give Stones as Gifts to Females," July 28, 2022, https://www.selwomarina.es/en/blog/por-que-pinguinos-regalan-piedras-hembra.

ABOUT THE AUTHOR

Anne Kertz Kernion, founder and artist of the inspirational greeting card company Cards by Anne, is an international lecturer and retreat leader. A former adjunct faculty member of Carlow University, Anne holds an MA in Theology from Duquesne University, a BS in Environmental Engineering from Penn State University, and a graduate certificate in Positive Psychology from the University of Missouri. She is the author of *A Year of Spiritual Companionship* and the award-winning *Spiritual Practices for the Brain*. Anne teaches yoga and enjoys biking and hiking. She and her husband Jack have three grown children and six grandchildren.